Finding You Finding Me

of related interest

Special Brothers and Sisters
Stories and Tips for Siblings of Children with a Disability
or Serious Illness
Edited by Annette Hames and Monica McCaffrey
ISBN 1 84310 383 4

"now you know me think more"
A Journey with Autism using Facilitated Communication Techniques
Ppinder Hundal and Pauline Lukey
ISBN 1 84310 144 0

A Strange World – Autism, Asperger's Syndrome
and PDD-NOS
A Guide for Parents, Partners, Professional Carers,
and People with ASDs
Martine F. Delfos
ISBN 1 84310 255 2

How to Live with Autism and Asperger Syndrome
Practical Strategies for Parents and Professionals
Chris Williams and Barry Wright
ISBN 1 84310 184 X

Growing Up Severely Autistic
They Call Me Gabriel
Kate Rankin
ISBN 1 85302 891 6
MIND Book of the Year 2001

People with Autism Behaving Badly
Helping People with ASD Move On from Behavioral
and Emotional Challenges
John Clements
ISBN 1 84310 765 1

Understanding Sensory Dysfunction
Learning, Development and Sensory Dysfunction
in Autism Spectrum Disorders, ADHD, Learning Disabilities
and Bipolar Disorder
Polly Godwin Emmons and Liz McKendry Anderson
ISBN 1 84310 806 2

Health Care and the Autism Spectrum
A Guide for Health Professionals, Parents and Carers
Alison Morton-Cooper
ISBN 1 85302 963 7

Finding You Finding Me

Using Intensive Interaction to get in touch
with people whose severe learning disabilities
are combined with autistic spectrum disorder

Phoebe Caldwell

Jessica Kingsley Publishers
London and Philadelphia

First published in 2006
by Jessica Kingsley Publishers
116 Pentonville Road
London N1 9JB, UK
and
400 Market Street, Suite 400
Philadelphia, PA 19106, USA

www.jkp.com

Library of Congress Cataloging in Publication Data
Caldwell, Phoebe.
     Finding you finding me : using intensive interaction to get in touch with people with severe
learning disabilities combined with autistic spectrum disorder / Phoebe Caldwell.— 1st american
pbk. ed.
          p. cm.
     Includes bibliographical references and index.
     ISBN-13: 978-1-84310-399-8 (pbk. : alk. paper)
     ISBN-10: 1-84310-399-0 (pbk. : alk. paper) 1. Autism—Patients—Rehabilitation. 2.
Nonverbal learning disabilities—Patients—Rehabilitation. I. Title.
     RC553.A88C35 2005
     616.85'88206—dc22
                                                                  2005015442

British Library Cataloguing in Publication Data
A CIP catalogue record for this book is available from the British Library

ISBN-13: 978 1 84310 399 8
ISBN-10: 1 84310 399 0

Printed and Bound in Great Britain by
Athenaeum Press, Gateshead, Tyne and Wear

Finding You Finding Me is dedicated
to the memory of Pranve.
He had the most beautiful smile.

Acknowledgements

I am extremely grateful to those people who have helped me, those who have given time to talk about ideas, especially Pete Coia and Nicholas Colloff, and Suzanne Zeedyk for involving me in the Dundee–Bergen University Seminar Group from whom I have learned much about the parallels between Intensive Interaction and Infant Imitation. I also need to thank Pavilion Publishers for generously allowing me to quote from my previous books *Person to Person* (Caldwell 1998), *You Don't Know What It's Like* (Caldwell 2000) and *Crossing the Minefield* (Caldwell 2002a) and also to use material from the training videos *Learning the Language* (Caldwell 2002b) and *Creative Conversations* (Caldwell 2005), all published by them. I should also like to thank those who have shared their lives with me, especially Christopher, Pranve and Gabriel, who are the mainspring of this book and who have taught me so much. Sadly, Pranve has died since this book was written.

Contents

CHAPTER 1

Introduction

What is this book about?

Finding You Finding Me is about some of the many people with whom I have been involved over the last 35 years, whose severe learning difficulties are linked with autism. While the majority are adult, some are children. Without exception, all those mentioned are on the autistic spectrum.

For those of us who are sometimes known as neurotypical (NT), who live with and support people on the spectrum, there is almost always a feeling of separation. In some respects this can be enhanced by definitions which separate 'us' and 'them' into categories – when the aim of this book is to show how we can share common ground. Nevertheless, 'neurotypical' is a convenient shorthand which is offered by people with autism and so I shall use it gratefully, while remembering that we have common purpose which I shall try to unravel as we move on. I shall think of us as partners with common purpose and endeavour.

How can we get in touch with each other? Where is the key to relationship in a partnership which will consist of one person who is known as autistic and the other who may be a parent, support partner, therapist, community worker, advocate, manager or simply someone who would like to be a friend but is baffled by the communication gulf? Since the two partners live in different sensory worlds, none of these roles will help us to meet unless we can find some way of getting close to each other which is comfortable for both of us.

Just as in the NT world, each person with autism is different. While there is a general umbrella term known as autistic spectrum disorder (ASD), it is very difficult to apply a set of specific rules to any one individual. For example, we cannot say 'Mary' is autistic and therefore she is afraid of being touched, since for her touch may be reassuring whereas for 'John' it may set off a wave of distasteful or painful sensation. Each person with ASD has their own sensory profile, differing from autistic person to person and completely different to that experienced by those of us who are neurotypical.

The first part of this book looks in detail at the sensory difficulties experienced by individuals who have ASD. Before we can help people on the spectrum we have to understand the sensory problems that are the day-to-day experience of their lives; otherwise we may be trying to engage with them in ways that increase their stress levels and make their condition worse.

Introducing Christopher, Pranve and Gabriel

Contrary to current practice, I have deliberately withheld the names of most of the individuals whose stories are told and have not invented alternative ones, because I want to focus on three people who I have worked with for varying lengths of time. In some sense this book is written for them. The particular stories of Christopher, Pranve and Gabriel are woven into the text. Even when talking about others, it holds them in mind.

At 43, Christopher is the oldest of the people I want to introduce. He is a large, gentle man who lives at home with his parents. He has a sister and enjoys her children. They love and interact with him. He goes to a day centre every day where I meet with him and his parents for about an hour. Christopher does not have speech. Occasionally he becomes distressed. This can sometimes be calmed by playing classical music.

Pranve is in his early twenties and lives with his mother and father. He finds it very difficult to relate to anyone and spends much of his time in retreat to a room of his own. He is hypersensitive to sound and his home is unfortunately near the edge of a busy airport. I am asked to see him because he is getting extremely disturbed. When he is upset he attacks people or bangs the walls in the hall. The first language spoken at home is English. He has minimal speech which is not easy to make out. It is proving virtually impossible to provide a service which will meet his needs. Together with the speech therapist, I visit him and his family for most of one day.

Gabriel lives in a residential college which supports many people with ASD. He has extreme autism and epilepsy and lives almost entirely in his own restless world, either flicking objects or quite often banging his head against the wall. He is already well known, since his mother has published *Growing Up Severely Autistic: They Call Me Gabriel* an interesting book about his life and the difficulties of finding adequate provision for him (Rankin 2000). Not having heard about this at the time, Gabriel and I were together for three days while we filmed a training video, *Learning the Language* (Caldwell 2002b).

Readers of earlier books (Caldwell 1998, 2000, 2002a) may find some of the other histories familiar. Where these have been included it is because they are landmarks which will help us to navigate a difficult terrain: the unfamiliar landscape experienced by people with ASD.

Intensive Interaction

The second half of *Finding You Finding Me* looks at the approach known as Intensive Interaction. Intensive Interaction uses our partner's own non-verbal body language to get in touch with them. It was first introduced by Gary Ephraim, then Principal Psychologist at Harperbury Hospital (Ephraim 1986), one of the large old hospitals for people with learning disability. Originally he called it 'Augmented Mothering'. Aware that the approaches he was using were not always effective in establishing communication, especially in people with severe learning disabilities and ASD, one day he tried echoing back a person's behaviour and was surprised when the individual sat up and started taking notice. So he tried the same approach with others, equally successfully. The headmaster of the hospital school was Dave Hewett who was very impressed by the marked improvement in these people's ability to communicate and in their behaviour. Renaming the process 'Intensive Interaction', Dave and Melanie Nind developed the approach with the children in Harperbury Hospital School. Their book *Access to Communication* is an account of five years of successfully using their approach with children in school (Nind and Hewett 1994).

I first came across Intensive Interaction when Gary was my supervisor for four years during the tenure of a Rowntree Fellowship working with adults. Previously I had been working on developing equipment individually designed to capture a person's attention. The idea of always basing an approach on what it was that held the person's interest dovetailed well with Ephraim's approach. From him, however, I learned that if I used a person's body language, I was the best piece of equipment that I had.

Similar techniques have arisen in other countries. In Aalberg, there is an institute where all deaf-blind children born in Denmark are educated using the same method introduced by the Director, Inge Rodbroe under the title 'Co-Creative Communication' – a name that rightly focuses on the contributions of both partners to the interactions (Nafstad and Rodbroe 1999). This is also used by Paul Hart (2004) in his work with deaf-blind children in Scotland. Fundamental research in France by Nadel simply calls the approach 'Imitation' and this term is used by many psychologists working in the field of infant development (Nadel and Camaioni 1993). In the context of Intensive Interaction I prefer not to use the word 'imitation'. This is because, in lay terms, the 'mimicking' and 'copying' which we associate with imitation carry childhood associations, some of which are unpleasant. Since I was mainly working with adults, management still raised the spectre that an approach with such a name cannot be respectful or age-appropriate. When I am teaching, I find it easier to encourage support staff to think of the approach as learning the basic elements of a person's language and using these to respond, since this cuts out any perceived element of manipulation. In normal conversation, when we talk to each other, we do not just copy, we answer.

There are elements of the Son-Rise Technique used in the US which are similar to Intensive Interaction. With Son-Rise the emphasis is on using the technique within a particular designated space, a special room which cuts out distraction. However, the experience of practitioners using Intensive Interaction suggests that the brain is so captivated when it recognizes its own signals that it has never been necessary to withdraw to a special place. The partner picks up their 'own signals from elsewhere' almost immediately. Even in their fifties, people who have never interacted before will sit up and start to communicate when they hear or see their sounds or movements. Their 'language' acts like a magnet to iron filings and because their brain recognizes its own sounds and movements, the person starts to attend to the world outside their own inner world.

Those practitioners who use Intensive Interaction may come to it with slightly different viewpoints. Nind and Hewett (1994) emphasize the underlying importance of the child–mother relationship. At the time I was introduced to the technique by Gary Ephraim, attention of providing services was heavily focused on delivering normalization. Although in practical terms this clearly had limitations when it came to working with highly disturbed adults, the theoretical climate was not receptive to an approach which management felt was age-inappropriate, especially as it was still called 'Augmented Mothering' by some. There were particular problems for people with ASD, since the sensory reality they experienced was anything but normal – care practices that were appropriate for neurotypicals were quite often totally unsuitable for a person with ASD. One only has to think of the natural urge to make homes bright and cheerful to realize this difficulty. I remember a community home where the team leader was engaged in a daily battle with a woman with ASD who removed the pictures from the walls. As she took them down, he put them up again, saying that she must have pictures on the wall (which were causing her sensory overload) because it was normal. I was asked to see her because she was exhibiting disturbed behaviour!

With the closing of some of the big hospitals it gradually became apparent that no matter how well-intentioned the staff and how user-friendly their new community homes, there was a core of people who were not able to settle and whose difficult behaviour persisted or even got worse. In houses with small rooms it was no longer possible for support staff to simply ignore this and the climate had swung against wholesale medication. Behavioural approaches did not always work. Staff were getting injured. Another approach was needed.

When support staff witness the use of the approach known as Intensive Interaction, they are often puzzled as to how it is possible to get to know people in such a short time, particularly those whose behaviour is very distressed and who have regular outbursts, inflicting harm on themselves or others, or who are very withdrawn. After all it would be difficult enough for those of us without ASD to feel close to each other, to feel in touch with a person's deepest feelings, to experience what can sometimes only be termed as intimacy, when we have hardly had time to meet. Even if the meeting has gone well, what possible benefit can come from such a lightning encounter?

And yet there is nothing miraculous about the approaches employed and described in this book. We can all use them if we focus on what it is that has meaning for the partner we are with and work through their language, the way they talk to themselves. But first of all I need to define what I mean when I use the term 'feeling'.

Digression into the world of 'feeling'

I am going to be talking a great deal about 'feeling'. This is an extremely slippery word as it has so many different meanings which only become evident in their context. We all use it. Scientists are discomforted by the idea of a non-quantifiable phenomenon that is difficult to measure. It is perceived as not objective although, using current scanning techniques, it is now possible to see that when we process what we see as emotion in others, we may be using our right-hand amygdala, a small walnut-sized organ in the brain. The amygdala used to be thought of as being just an early warning system that processed stimuli that were perceived as potentially dangerous, but recent work suggests that, at least under some circumstances, it may be involved in the processing of a wider range of emotions (Pegna *et al.* 2005).

The word 'feeling' comes in all shapes and sizes.

'I feel the chair I am sitting on' is a simple description of the physical sensation of pressure experienced by my back and backside.

'I feel angry' says something about my emotional state when I am aware of a rising tide of arousal as my hormonal response to a distasteful situation swings into action.

When I say 'I feel you are angry' – which may shade into 'I feel you are angry with me' – I am probably picking up subliminal clues from your body language. But at this stage it may be that it is I who am angry – but, unable to bear this, I project my state on to you. I am ascribing to you feelings which are properly mine. Projection is something we all do and we need to be on the look-out for this tendency, since it not only affects the people we work with but also can affect the way we work.

Feelings are not black and white; they shade off into each other. 'I feel the chair' (physical sensation) may slide into fear (emotion) if, for example, I am leaning back and I lean back too far. As the chair threatens to tip over, my feeling slides from tactile sensation and proprioceptive feelings of imbalance to panic, an emotional response to a potentially life-threatening situation.

The odd thing is that everything we experience has its 'quota of feeling' although we may not notice it. I became very aware of this when I was teaching. I asked a student to describe a sofa she had designed. She told me its colour and dimensions and then her voice changed as she waved her arms and said, 'I wanted it to be warm and comfortable.'

Immediately we were transported from the world of a green two-seater to the affective world of all the possibilities of nurturing containment and burgeoning relationships. If we can learn to develop our awareness of the affective content of each situation, it is like moving from black and white to colour or shifting a dimension. What we have to do is to learn to pay attention to our feeling responses. This allows us to be far more creative in our interactions and relationships with each other. It requires practice and deliberate focusing and exploration but the effort repays dividends in our ability to get in touch with others. With his permission I quote an example given by Pete Coia which he uses to help students analyse their thoughts and behaviour (Coia 2004).

The student is asked to imagine they are standing on a station and the train is late. What do they feel? It may be that they are meeting someone they love and their day implodes. On the other hand it may be they have to go to a meeting they don't want to and they feel relieved to have got out of it.

At this point I want to carry this example even further and ask the student to tell me about the physical components of the sensation. What does perceived catastrophe or relief 'feel like'? This may seem a long way off from autism but it is by becoming attentive to the warmth and the tightness and prickliness, palpitations and sweat that we learn how we truly feel. This helps us to develop attention to others and not to project our feelings onto them. In order to meet others we also have to learn to listen to the good and rough bits of ourselves, particularly 'without judgement'. As soon as we start being judgemental about how we feel, we impose limits on ourselves and suppress the bits we don't like, while at the same time projecting our boundaries onto other people. This distorts all the possibilities of knowing each other as we are.

To look at all this from the point of dealing with how we feel, we can do one of three things. We can bury our feeling in ourselves, switching off and resolutely refusing to look at a feeling which is too painful (repression). In this case we sever connection with the feeling by hiding it. Second, we can embrace it with all its pain and reward. Third, we can hide ourselves from the source of the feeling by retreating into our inner world, the route that is most often used by those with ASD and severe learning disabilities when their sensory intake is too painful.

All this can cause confusion if we are not aware of it. On the whole I shall use the term 'sensation' to describe physical feelings, 'emotion' in the normal accepted sense, and 'affect' where perception of the state or feelings of another object or person is involved.

Whose reality?

To come back to Christopher: At the day centre he sits by a table looking at his left hand. He holds it close to his nose and inspects the palm with great care. Apparently oblivious to the activities going on round him, he closes his fingers to a fist and continues to examine this with deep attention. His right hand is clenched tightly under his vest, screwing the interlocked material in his fingers. This is what he does.

Christopher has autism. For those of us who do not, who are 'neurotypical', it is difficult for us to make sense of what he is doing and why he is doing it. What is so fascinating about his left hand and why does he cling so desperately to his vest? Why is he so withdrawn from us?

Whether we are autistic or NT we all experience a different reality, a different set of blueprints depending both on our inherited characteristics and what happens to us. We all see life through our own particular lenses so that in spite of our shared reality we react in our own particular way. One of the hard life lessons we learn is that other people's reality needs to be respected as valid for them.

To understand what is going on for people with ASD, we have to let go of our own sensory reality – the world we experience – and enter an alternative dimension, where what we see, feel, hear, taste and smell is presented to us in a completely different way to that which we are used to, to what those of us who are NT call 'normal'. If we have ASD, it is not that our senses will be faulty – but rather the way that the information that does reach our senses is subsequently processed. We who are NT have to place ourselves in (for us) an alien world where nothing quite makes sense. Events that we take for granted as part and parcel of our normal daily lives may be confusing or even painful for those on the autistic spectrum.

One of the aims of this book is to explore the sensory reality experienced by people like Christopher, Pranve and Gabriel so that we can begin to understand why they are doing things that may seem bizarre to us but are totally logical within the context of the autistic experience. To do this, we are helped by being able to visit the accounts of people with autism who are writing, speaking and making videos that tell us about their world.

Fortunately there are now a number of these and the story they tell us is consistent. Among others, we owe a particular debt to Donna Williams, Gunilla Gerland, Therese Jolliffe, Lindsey Weeks, Temple Grandin and Ros Blackburn. Wendy Lawson's book *Build Your Own Life* (2003), which explores the reality of the NT world from the point of view of a person with ASD and Asperger's Syndrome, is especially interesting. I also owe a great debt in understanding to Gail Gillingham (who is NT) for her work on the structure of autism and her insightful work on the hypersensitivities (Gillingham 1995, 2000).

Objections have been raised in the past that the brain of a person on the autistic spectrum is malfunctioning, therefore their accounts lack value. This is to look at ASD from our NT point of view which tells us that only what we see from the outside can be objective. Besides which, unless we wire people up to scanners we cannot measure sensation and, even if we could, it still doesn't tell us *how this person feels*. And it dismisses completely the consistency of these extraordinary accounts from widely different parts of the world, which not only lead us into the world of autism, but in doing so shed light on the whole art of learning what it is to be with 'other' – and what this means in terms of being human. Taken together with the possibilities opened up by the approach known as Intensive Interaction, our journey will be through the landscape of feeling, one of discovery, emotional enlargement and hope, both for our partners with ASD and ourselves.

From an NT point of view we see Christopher as cut off from us, lost in his inaccessible world. In the day centre, activities go on round him, but when I saw him, he appeared to be taking no part. But how does he see our world or, rather, how does he experience the people and the environment around him? Does he, like Lindsey Weeks as a child, feel himself to be 'an alien in a foreign land' (Weeks Undated) or 'an imposter in that other solar system' (Williams 1995)?

And what is Christopher's relationship between his inner world and the NT world that we share? Why is his attention focused so deeply in the sensatory feedback he is deriving from the texture of his vest?

We need to pay great attention to what the authors with ASD are telling us. These are the experts. If we do not we shall find ourselves making behavioural judgements and basing our strategies on our NT experience of reality and not that which is experienced by people with ASD.

ASD and learning disabilities?

But we also do have to remember that these writers are living at the able end of the spectrum. Although the nearest we are going to get to understanding the reality experienced by people with severe learning disabilities and ASD is through their words, in some ways this is like building half a bridge – a torrent still separates us from the far shore. To get to the other side we are going to have to rely on the sometimes wobbly stepping stones of our own observations of behaviour and responses. How does *this* person with intellectual disability react when I do such-and-such?

I repeat, we must also remember that each individual who has autism is first and foremost an individual. *Not everything that is said about people with ASD, even if said by those who have ASD themselves, will apply to all the others who have it.* Donna Williams is clear about this. In her film *Jam-Jar*, she says, 'I am not a spokesperson for all the people with autism. Here is Johnny, look at him and learn from him' (Williams 1995).

One of the concepts I have found most useful in exploring our separate points of view is Donna's idea of 'her world' and 'the world'. In this book I shall use the terms *inner world* and *outer world* to avoid confusion. In her revealing book *Nobody Nowhere*, Donna gives us a vivid account of her retreat from 'the world' to a place where she could 'lose [herself] in anything [she] desired' (Williams 1999a).

But inner and outer worlds are not exclusive to people with autism. They are common to all of us. In my inner world I can reflect, think, plan, dream and daydream. It is a storehouse for the good and bad experiences which set the patterns of my life. As an NT, my attention is mostly on interaction with the world outside. But on the whole my outside world experience is benign. I sympathize with and believe Wendy Lawson

(2003) but do not share her experience when she says, 'the more I become aware of the world around me the more I am afraid'.

Unlike Donna and Wendy and Therese Jolliffe, barring natural disasters I do not normally experience the world as hostile. Threat is not my day-to-day norm. I do not have to run away like Donna, who in her penetrating poem 'Nobody Nowhere' (Williams 1999a) says that she has to 'run away to the corners of her mind' – a profoundly moving description of the retreat into the inner world.

However, at this point we need to consider the thorny question of whether or not people with ASD *do* have intellectual learning disabilities. This doubt arises mainly because some of the effects of the hyper-sensitivities experienced by people with ASD are so confusing and painful that those who experience them withdraw almost completely into their own inner worlds. Here they can focus on self-stimulus to the exclusion of the stimuli from the outer world which they find so distressing. Even the most able may have delayed speech development and *appear* to have learning disabilities but with suitable support learn to function well in 'our world'. There are some who contend that no-one with ASD has a learning disability and their problems are entirely a function of their autism.

Although it may be an artificial distinction, most of what is known about people with ASD is learned from those who are known as 'high-functioning' – that is, they understand what is said to them but cannot process an answer. Therese Jolliffe speaks about 'the awful frustration of not being able to say what [she] want[s], how [she] want[s] to scream and break things and sometimes to hit people' (Jolliffe, Lansdown and Robinson 1992).

Those who are known as 'low-functioning' seem to us neither able to process their intake or organize a reply.

Almost all research focuses entirely on the more able people with ASD, for the obvious reason that it is easier for us to communicate with them. However, if we ask the question as to whether learning disabilities and autism are connected the other way round, we see that there are many people with learning disabilities who are diagnosed as being on the spectrum of what is known as autism. Conversely, there are a number of people with learning disabilities who *are* on the autistic spectrum but who never get diagnosed, because their behaviour is attributed to their learning disability. Because of the stigma that unfortunately still attaches itself to learning disabilities, such people are in danger of being invisible. For these people, on top of the sensory processing difficulties experienced by people with autism they may have other severe cognitive disabilities. In their case, the battles of their autism are being fought over ground which is in itself a war zone. Because the voice of people at the able end of the autistic spectrum is so powerful, there is the danger that those who are intellectually impaired will be denied existence. They must not be ignored just because they have no voice. They are just as much in need of our help, if not more so, as those who have ASD without cognitive impairment. Focusing on their deep hypersensitivities to physical sensory stimuli may be a more profitable line of research to help them, rather than on cognitive deficit. But above all they are people whose behaviour frequently indicates extreme distress and with whom we urgently need to learn to communicate.

The next problem is that it is extremely difficult to tell into which group a person falls by just looking at them. Because of the sensory distress they are experiencing, almost all people with ASD will have withdrawn to a state which excludes any interventions they may have been offered. They may be non-verbal like Christopher, Pranve and Gabriel. For example, at the time of writing I do not know if Christopher can understand what I am saying to him, although some of his responses suggest that he probably can. The most effective way of working with him will be to try and lower his stress level to see how far we can develop trust and get to know each other, how well we can communicate. If we can lift a corner of the curtain of autism, then we can begin to see how effectively his brain can function.

Developing interaction

Intensive Interaction is mostly used with people who are non-verbal or on the borderlines of speech. Although it works across a broad spectrum of disability, it appears to be particularly effective with people on the autistic spectrum. In looking at how a person talks to themselves and using this to develop conversation, we can begin to shift their attention from solitary self-stimulation to shared activity with the world outside. Once we have got past the idea that what we may be doing is not part of our 'normal repertoire' and may be witnessed as 'odd' by the onlooker, this is an astonishingly successful way of building relationships. The outcome can be a tremendous flowering of the capacity of communication partners to be with each other, in a way that will change not only 'difficult to live with' behaviour but also addresses the priorities in our own lives.

What is it that is really important to us during this short period we are together? For me, I want to feel good about myself and help others feel good about themselves. That seems to be the best I can do. 'You cannot change someone's autism but you can change the way in which an individual can cope with it' (Beardon 2004).

However, we really can also change the lives of our partners with ASD if we are prepared to lay aside the reality that we experience and learn to interact through a language that has meaning for them.

But before we can go on to discuss the positive approaches associated with Intensive Interaction, we need to look more closely at the particular sensory problems faced by people whose learning disabilities are compounded by ASD.

CHAPTER 2

What is Autism?

This is a difficult question to answer at present. We can talk about its effects, which are summarized in what is known as the 'Triad of Impairments' – that is, a failure to understand speech, a failure in the capacity to build relationships and also to have the capacity for flexible thought. However, although it is a useful diagnostic tool, the Triad sees people in terms of failure. It does nothing to help us understand how it is that people who have ASD experience their world. (In a burst of humour which a person with autism is not 'supposed' to possess, a speaker at a conference proposed an alternative Triad – that of failure by the educational system, the social services and NHS.) What is clear is that the term ASD covers a very wide spectrum of conditions both in degree and spread. For a list of some of the current ideas about the origin of ASD see Appendix A.

What does autism feel like?

Because autism so easily leads to a breakdown in communication and hence what we call challenging behaviour, there is a danger that we think of it in terms of the management difficulties it poses us. How can we relate to or provide a service for people who appear cut off from us and who demonstrate behaviours which, according to our world, are bizarre, self-harming or sometimes randomly aggressive? They seem to want no part of our world. Even in well-intentioned services the question often boils down to how they can be contained. Families may be at their wits' end – and sometimes feeling guilty at their despair. Struggling with financial pressures, I meet staff who are being asked to cope with impossible levels of aggression and management who are unable to come up with solutions. In many cases, person-centred planning is interpreted as how we can fit individuals into our agendas. Quite a number of the people in the most deep distress are boys fighting their way through the hormonal jungle of puberty.

Whatever the underlying causes, looking at it from this viewpoint does not give us a clear picture of what it *feels like* to have ASD. To try and get a clearer idea, Luke Beardon suggests a Triad of Support (Beardon 2004):

1. time spent with an individual trying to see the world through their eyes

2. understanding the theory, the ways in which people with ASD learn and process

3. combining these and putting theory into practice.

If we are lucky, the study of individual behaviours may enable us to stand back and get glimpses of the wider picture.

We can spend time with Donna Williams through studying the images in the fascinating film, *Jam-Jar* (1995). Here we see Donna walking down the crisps aisle of a supermarket. She passes the different coloured packets but is not able to process the image of one before her eyes have picked up the next one. This second image is still unprocessed by the time she sees the third and so on down the line. She says:

> As I pass the shelves, my eyes see everything without processing them...my eyes are flooded with this big array of contrasts...as I walk away from each place the impressions from the last one are still caught in my head.

Successive images swirl around her brain in an unprocessed 'overload'. For those of us who do not experience this it is helpful if we can give ourselves a concrete image, a model that we can actually hold in our minds. The effect seems to be something like a busy airport where more airplanes come in than there is space for them to land on the runway, so they stack up.

Overload

If we push our model further, under these conditions, an air traffic controller will see too many blips on his radar screen. These will start to overlap and interfere with each other. In the same way, the brain of someone with ASD has too many images or sounds or other sensory impressions swirling around. There appears to be a bottleneck in the processing system causing 'overload'. Wendy Lawson (2003) tells us that overload 'is uncomfortable and causes [her] pain'.

In an article in the *Sunday Telegraph*, Temple Grandin talks about the difficulties of filtering out distractions: 'All the zillions of sensory details in the world come into our consciousness and we are overwhelmed by the swirling mass of tiny detail.'

So, let us imagine we can see and hear everything, and everything has equal weight and importance. Nothing stands out. We can't catch hold of a particular thread. To test this, just try listening. You will probably, if you are sitting like I am at a computer, hear its cosy hum. You may also hear a clock ticking and almost certainly a background of traffic noise. There may be bird song or the noise of sheep baaing. The point of this is that the NT system has learned to operate on a 'need to know' basis, and has learned to filter out almost everything it does not need to know. It has become totally selective to those aspects of its life that it deems to be worthy of notice. It attends to those that are and withdraws attention from those that are not, in order to protect itself from overload. While a more able person with ASD may be able to make a more conscious selection in order to keep up with the important threads of what is going on, for the less able there is no such option. They can quite literally drown in over-stimulation.

Overload can also arise when two or more messages conflict. For example, this can happen if a person has learned how to do a particular activity but has not been able to learn what happens if not all the conditions for doing it are present. I might have learned how to lay out the tea but, because no-one has emptied the dishwasher, I find there are no mugs. The message 'put the cups on the table' conflicts with the situational message 'there are no cups in the cupboard'. I cannot resolve the conflict and my brain goes into overload, desperately seeking a way out.

Fragmentation

Worse is to come. As when there are too many stacked-up airplanes, eventually there will be a crash. All the sensory images will start to break up, a process known as 'fragmentation'. Gunilla Gerland, Donna Williams and Lindsey Weeks paint a picture of fragmentation as a number of extremely unpleasant and terrifying sensations. Fragmentation can be associated with pain, confusion and sometimes heat, a combination which gives rise to the suspicion that part of the autonomic nervous system is running riot. Lindsey says that he would do anything to avoid it: 'run in front of a car, or bash [his] head against a wall' (Weeks Undated).

Possibly it is something akin to the effects experienced in a panic attack. A little boy's mother asks me why he keeps on crying, 'My head's running away, my head's running away!' I try to explain to her that this is not some odd hallucination but, almost certainly, a very accurate description of how the onset of overload and fragmentation feels for him.

Coping strategies

Because of the terrifying sensations they will be subject to, the one thing that people with ASD want to avoid at any cost is moving from overload to fragmentation. In order to avoid this, they tend to develop coping strategies to reduce the stress they experience so that they can maintain a sense of coherence. Traditionally these coping strategies have been seen as undesirable and steps have been taken to try to reduce them directly. Usually the word 'Don't!' features in such programmes.

These coping strategies fall roughly into two groups. The first is that the person withdraws into themselves and focuses on a particular physical sensation, object or theme. These repetitive behaviours, which are a very noticeable feature of people with severe autism, may be as simple as concentrating on their own breathing rhythm, tearing paper, arranging furniture or switching lights on and off. One of the commonest ways people self-stimulate is by rubbing their fingers together in different ways. In addition to his sounds, Pranve does this. In Christopher's case, he inspects his fingers and also wraps his other hand tightly in the material of his vest. It looks as if the feedback he is giving himself is through vision and touch. Concentrating on these simple sensations helps to reduce the amount of processing his brain has to do since it cuts down on the number of stimuli he has to take on board. From the point of view of a person with autism, at least there is something here that has meaningful cause and effect.

Others may fixate on physical activities such as running and bouncing. Certainly some of the more violent repetitive behaviours work directly by promoting the production of endorphins in the brain, which calm its overactivity and allow it to concentrate more on what is happening. For some people, watching particular videos or taking part in even more complex activities and themes, to the exclusion of the world about them, narrows down the field of sensory intake, so reducing the amount of sensory processing required.

Alternatively, the person may try and get out of the situation which is overloading them directly, using an exit strategy such as shutting or hiding their eyes, pulling their shirts over their heads or running away. A schoolboy pulls a blanket over his head to shut out the stimuli he cannot process. The alternative to this tactic of avoidance is to try to reduce the amount of disturbing stimulus that is flooding the brain by getting rid of the perceived source. In such cases they may attack the person with them in order to get them to go away. In their desperation to hasten our departure, they may kick, bite, spit, pinch, push and head-butt, all the behaviours we find so difficult to manage and also, in many cases, strike us as personal rejection. However, our first response must be to look at whether or not we are overloading them with stimuli. For example, just the presence of people can be enough to trigger overload without their actually doing anything.

Perhaps more subtly than direct attack, Ros Blackburn (2004) tells us that she used to 'throw the handbag of [her] keyworker out of the window'. One can imagine that seeing her credit cards floating down the street was a very effective way of persuading her key worker to depart.

Fight/flight response

Much of what we see as 'difficult behaviour' in people with ASD seems to be related either to the aggression or withdrawal associated with trying to prevent themselves getting overloaded to the point of tipping into fragmentation. In the twin responses of avoidance and aggression we recognize the body's primary defence system against danger – what is known as the fight/flight response. This is the basic survival mechanism which we all have. It helps protect us when we feel threatened. (If I see a snake, I might hit it or run away.) One of the most important ideas we need to bear in mind is that, if the senses are feeding in stimuli which appear threatening (in the case of ASD because they are not being processed properly, together with the associated fear that the brain will plunge headlong into fragmentation with all its horrible effects), then the threshold for triggering the fight/flight response may be zero. The person gets the feeling of incipient disaster, that they are being attacked even if they are not – and so they respond as such, either by running away or lashing out. This is made worse if, in addition, the person has a low level of self-esteem. They simply do not have the wherewithal to stand up to the level of overloading stimuli.

Occasionally a person will go into a third mode of defence, equivalent to 'freeze'. I have seen two people with severe ASD go catatonic, unable to move. One was trapped in unstoppable laughter, her body rigid and eyes fixed to the ceiling. This had nothing to do with anything funny. When she was distressed, the other simply froze up completely, sometimes for hours.

Inducing stress

Experience of using Intensive Interaction suggests that whether or not the person's brain will become so overloaded that all the sounds, sensations and images break up (with all the distressing sensations associated with this process) is determined by how 'stressed' a person is at the time. This seems to be absolutely central.

Although we can recognize ourselves in some of the situations that cause stress in people with ASD, for them the majority of their distress is *not* caused by the same events that we find disturbing. More often it relates to environmental issues that we would experience as benign, such as certain frequencies or particular colours and especially people. We can reduce this stress by reducing sensory input they find disturbing on the one hand and, on the other, giving them significant markers in our world, which are meaningful to them since they are drawn from the language of their inner world (the way they talk to themselves). Their brain now has an alternative to focus on rather than their sensory distress. Using this twofold approach we can go a long way to preventing people getting too overloaded and tipping into fragmentation. Time and again when we use Intensive Interaction, we see people relax as they begin to find they can relate to the outside world through a language that has meaning for them. Their faces clear; their bodies relax. They stop focusing on their inner world and, instead of appearing simply to reject the world outside, look up and round at their surroundings calmly. As we shall see, the brain appears to function better in terms of its ability to process.

Descriptions of fragmentation

Compare two of the descriptions of what it feels like to go into fragmentation by Donna Williams and Gunilla Gerland, two different people coming from the opposite ends of the world. To us they sound bizarre, but taken together, we seem to be looking at a very specific neurological description of the onset sensations of fragmentation.

Gunilla tells us that when she was growing up she suffered

> an almost constant shudder in [her] spine which periodically grew worse. It was a constant torture, most noticeable when it changed in intensity... It was like feeling the moment before you sneeze, only as if that had got stuck. (Gerland 1996)

She continues:

> It was like cold steel down my spine. It was hard and fluid at the same time with metallic fingers drumming on the outside. Like sharp clips digging into my spine and *lemonade* inside. Icy heat and digging fire inside. It was like the sound of screeching chalk against a blackboard turned into a silent concentration of feeling, then placed in the back of my neck. From there, so metallic, the feeling rang in my ears, radiated out into my arms and clipped itself firmly into my elbows. (Gerland 1996)

Donna Williams gives us an horrific account of how she experienced fragmentation as a child:

> A feeling kept washing over me. It began with the feeling one gets from *eating lemons*. It was like a tingling in the back of the neck. It spread to every fiber of my body like cracks in an earthquake. I knew this monster. It was the Big Black nothingness and it felt like death coming to get me. The walls went up and my ears hurt. I had to get out, out of the room, out of this thing stuck on me, suffocating me inside my shell of flesh. A scream rose in my throat. My four year old legs ran from one side of the room, moving ever faster and faster, my body hitting the wall like a sparrow flying at the window. My body was shaking. Here it was. Death was here. Don't want to die, don't

want to die, don't want to die…the repetition of the words blended
into a pattern with only one word standing out, the word die. My
knees went to the floor. My hands ran down the mirror. My eyes fran-
tically searched the eyes looking back, looking for meaning, looking
for something to connect. No-one, nothing, nowhere. Silent screaming rose in my throat. My head seemed to explode. My chest heaved
with each final breath at the gates of death. Dizziness and exhaustion
began to overtake the terror. It was amazing how many times a day I
could be dying and still be alive. (Williams 1999a)

In both of these accounts we have a very specific description, that one of
the first signs of the onset of fragmentation is a feeling in the back of the
neck, as a woman with Asperger's Syndrome also put it, like 'fizzy
lemonade'. If this is so it is not surprising that quite often one of the signs a
person is getting upset is that they rub or beat the back of the neck in order
to try and desensitize themselves from what appears to be a neuro-
biological sensation which they recognize – and dread what it heralds as it
spreads through their body.

A young man is living in a hospital because his behaviour has deterio-
rated to the point at which it needs several people to cope with his
outbursts. When these are coming on, the first sign is that he stands, rubs
the back of his head and his neck and then beats the back of his neck.
Sometimes a cold wet towel applied to the neck helps to desensitize him.

In another very specific respect, Lindsey Weeks' account tallies with
Donna's. Like Donna, Lindsey also experienced a repetitive word which
repeated itself over and over. Demonstrating this on the tape *A Bridge of
Voices*, we hear him repeating the word, 'pain, *pain*, **pain**' over and over
again until it appears to engulf him (Weeks Undated).

Looking for meaning

As their world falls apart (in that a person can no longer rely on their senses
to present them with a coherent and meaningful picture) they may fall
back to a second line of defence, desperately looking for coherence, trying
to cling on to at least something which they recognize and can focus on.
Donna tells us that she used to look in the mirror, looking for visual confirmation, peering into the eyes looking back to see if there was some feature

they could still recognize, that made sense – no-one, nothing, nowhere (Williams 1999a).

When she heard a particular sound, Gunilla clung to the fence beside her. If she hung on there was at least one sensation she could interpret: 'Up and down were suddenly in the same place. I had no idea where my feet were' (Gerland 1996).

Perhaps those of us who have lost our sense of balance after an attack of influenza and crawled along the floor, clinging to the floorboards because it's the only feeling we can recognize, may have some idea of the sensations she was experiencing on a regular basis.

The different senses may be affected to a different degree in different people. Some people seem to be able to hang on to and make sense of tactile sensations, long after the rest of their world is swirling about. A small boy loves his fluffy rabbit but is denied the opportunity to take it to school; his mother feels it is unsuitable. At school, where he spends much of his time cowering beneath a table, I persuade him to draw a rabbit. He comes out. Together we draw and colour and mount a splendid rabbit which I put on his desk and tell him he can have it at any time. He starts to wander about the classroom. After a little while the commotion becomes too much for him and we can see the tension is beginning to rise in him. Suddenly he swings round and says, 'Be good, hold Rabbit.'

When his world is breaking up, 'Rabbit' is an island of stability. When he clings to his rabbit, *he knows what he is doing.* If he holds on to Rabbit, his brain recognizes the sensation of touch. But at school even a drawn image of his rabbit is enough to stabilize him. The familiar brain–body conversation orientates him and helps him to stem the tide of disintegration, to hang on to at least a portion of the reality which we so lightly take for granted.

A young man walks about with a clothes peg on his finger. It is useful to try this. Close your eyes and squeeze your index finger hard between the thumb and index finger of the other hand. Focus on the sensation because, as your sense of coherence falls apart, it is the only sensation in the world that is meaningful. If you concentrate on this powerful feedback, you can cut out everything else.

Gail Gillingham points out in her fascinating book *Autism – Handle with Care* (1995) that if we remove the objects of a person's fascination we take away the protection they have developed to guard themselves, leaving them vulnerable to the pains of fragmentation. We have to learn to work through a person's behaviours and fixations rather than against them. Temple Grandin (tape) tells us that if a person loves airplanes and we want to teach them to read, we need to stick the letters on the pictures of the planes.

Fixations

Just how urgent the attachment is to an object of fixation was brought home to me by a young man who collected leaves in bottles. One day in the autumn he was in a state of extreme distress when a mower ploughed straight through a pile of fallen leaves. He ran past shouting, 'They're cutting up my friends, they're killing all my friends!'

In our reality this may seem an extreme reaction, but as far as he was concerned, his entire life-support system was being destroyed. His friends, his allies, all that he depended on for a sense of knowing what he was doing, for a sense of coherence, was being wiped out and he was being left defenceless.

In the book *There's a Boy in Here* (Barron and Barron 1992), Sian Barron tells us: 'he loved turning the lights on and off because it gave him a wonderful sense of security. He knew what would happen, it was exactly the same each time.'

Temple Grandin (tape) says that, as a child, 'I was intensely preoccupied with the sound of a spinning coin, it cut out all the other sounds. Even quite loud sounds did not disturb me.'

If you fix on a particular sensation it can at least be something to hang on to in a fragmented, turning, kaleidoscope world where, as Therese Jolliffe (Jolliffe *et al.* 1992) tells us, '[she] spend[s] [her] whole life trying to make sense of what is happening and the pattern never settles'.

Behaviour we see as bizarre may literally be the life-blood and life-support system of someone with ASD who is battling to make out the pattern of what is happening. When it was suggested to a young man that he calmed down, he screamed at us in exasperation one day, 'You don't know what it's like, you don't know what it's like!' He could not tell us what it was like; it was the only time we heard him speak. That was 35 years ago and I have been wondering ever since. What is it like to inhabit a world which must be like living in a bowl of Mulligatawny soup with all the bits swirling round? No landmarks, no consistency and, when it all gets too much, pain. Blind Man's Bluff with the targets always on the move? What surprises me is not that people with ASD present behavioural problems for management but the remarkable grasp of logic they maintain within the parameters of their autism. If we can understand and work within each individual template, then we can begin to help them survive in and even enjoy our world – they can begin to relate to it without always feeling threatened. It is a journey in which both of us will be learners and both will be enriched.

What is *not* clear from the accounts from able people is the extent to which the acute physical pains of fragmentation moderate after adolescence, since there do not seem to be accounts of this type of extreme breakdown in adults in the literature. The only comparative reference I am able to find is that of Lindsey Weeks (Undated) who, when referring to fragmentation, says that, 'It's bad enough when you are an adult but when you are a child it's really scary.'

As for those whose severe learning disabilities are compounded by autism and who cannot speak for themselves, all we can do is judge from their behavioural responses to people and their environment. From the evidence of their sometimes extreme behavioural distress, one has to presume that many of them do continue experiencing fragmentation throughout adult life. They cannot help themselves through logic and communication: their only resort is to develop coping strategies, which can so often include severe aggression.

It is not unusual to hear support staff say, 'Oh, they'll get used to it.' This is completely to misunderstand the nature of ASD. The neuro-biological event which is at the root of autism does not go away, even if a proportion of the gifted people with ASD do learn to cope in an adult life which always has to struggle to interpret an alien world. We have to help them, by reducing the stimuli they find so unbearable and also by finding non-invasive ways of making connection with them (see Chapter 5 on Intensive Interaction).

CHAPTER 3

Causes of Stress

To return to Christopher in his day centre: when I try to explain to his parents how the things in the room might be swirling around, Christopher looks directly at me and laughs and holds out his hand in a gesture of agreement. Although it is too early to tell, I think he is one of the people with ASD who can process at least some of what is said. The question is: what is it that causes stress in his brain? How can we lower the stress level so that he is able to process more effectively?

The *Oxford Dictionary* defines 'stress' as 'tension which results from adverse circumstances'. The problem for people with ASD is that the brain presents certain aspects of our shared environment (some of which we may find pleasant and positive), and also some of their bodily feelings, as painful. For example, the nice, warm internal feedback we get when someone smiles at us is described as agony by Donna Williams (1999a). Again, the colourful stripey jersey we enjoy wearing may set off sensory overload in a person with ASD, with its threat of tipping them into fragmentation. No-one can understand why a man attacks his helper on certain days and not others, until it is realized that his outbursts coincide with the days his helper wears a black jersey with a white zig-zag. The disturbed behaviour stops when he no longer wears this particular pullover.

We who are NT may enjoy animated conversation. At the same time as listening to people's inflections we also watch their body language, even if we are not conscious of doing this. It adds colour to their words. Yet Wendy Lawson (2003) tells us that because of the inability of her brain to process more than a limited amount of information at one time, she cannot both listen and watch a person who is talking to her simultaneously. She is 'monotropic' – can only focus on and process one sensory input at a time – so to take in different modes of sensory stimuli simultaneously is stressful.

Many others find direct speech stressful and prefer to be addressed through indirect speech or to communicate indirectly through computer. It gives time to interpret and process.

Each person with ASD is different and will find different aspects of their environment trigger what Therese Jollife *et al.* (1992) describe as 'living in terror, not just of what is happening now but that something terrible *may* happen'.

It has been suggested that almost all the disturbed behaviour we experience in people with ASD can be traced back to hypersensitivities to their environment. Experiencing such a topsy-turvy world, one can see how hard it would be to know what is happening if one cannot rely on the evidence of one's senses. However, if we are going to subscribe to this way of looking at the onset of stress, we should also have to include hypersensitivity to internal feedback, such as the 'over-the-top' hormonal surges experienced by boys with ASD in puberty. In her incredibly helpful book *Autism – An Inside-Out Approach* (1996), Donna Williams describes the effects of such surges on the body: 'They [the person with ASD] feel as if they are being attacked and respond as such.'

Holding his head in his hands, a young man who is extremely disturbed said, 'I just wish someone would help me sort out my head.'

Hypersensitivities

It is difficult for we who are NT to appreciate what it means to be hypersensitive. It is outside our range, way off our sensory Richter Scale. How can we understand this? How can we bridge the credibility gap and understand a sensory reality so far removed from our own?

All of us, NT and autistic, share the same physical world – the same basic reality. We take this for granted – a three-dimensional environment with time as the fourth dimension. But scientists are now seriously telling us that in order to understand the cosmos they have to postulate at least ten dimensions. For most of us, imagination fails at this point. Our brains close the shutters and tell us this is nonsense; it cannot be so because we have no way of visualizing such a state. Although this may seem an extreme example, the principle is the same.

We who are NT have to find ways of taking on board that, in autism, stress really is caused by triggers which we who are NT find difficult to comprehend. They may be the same sort of events we find 'a bit much' but we have ways of cutting down on too much sensory input which do not draw attention to us. We can, so to speak, 'switch off', by focusing on something else or withdrawing. And although people with ASD, particularly those who are more able, may use these options, many are simply swamped by sensory intake which is too powerful or interpreted as hostile. Basically, it hurts too much.

However, placing ourselves outside our own level of experience is very difficult. In practice we are all living through our own realities, looking at a world planned out for us by our inheritance and experience, looking through our own special glasses of nature and nurture. What we have to do is to take off these spectacles and start taking on board what other people are telling us. So let us listen to the experts when they tell us what it is like to be hypersensitive.

A young man tells me:

> 'If you were hypersensitive to sound and stood beside me, you would hear the blood pumping in my veins.'

> 'The pain is worse than a rape alarm being let off inside your ear.'

Temple Grandin says, 'Light touch feels like a cattle prod.' She also tells us of a student, Holly, who is so sensitive to sound she hears the electric wires humming in the walls (Grandin and Scariano 1986).

Long before a plane appeared or could be heard in the sky, a young man I was working with would get excited and point to where it would eventually appear.

Perhaps a more objective indication of the severity of a hypersensitive response was given by a man with Asperger's Syndrome who also has kidney stones. These are notoriously painful. When he was asked by his surgeon to rate out of ten the comparative pain of his hypersensitivity to light to that of the stones which the surgeon was about to treat, the young man told us that he put 'the kidney stones at four and the pain of light sensitivity at seven to eight out of ten'.

We really have to make a blind leap to try to get the measure of what it is to be hypersensitive because it is evident that hypersensitivities are a major underlying factor in what we see (from our reality) as the disturbed behaviour in people with ASD, since they trigger the coping strategies needed to avoid going into overload and fragmentation. We need to look at these in more detail. (See Figure 3.1.)

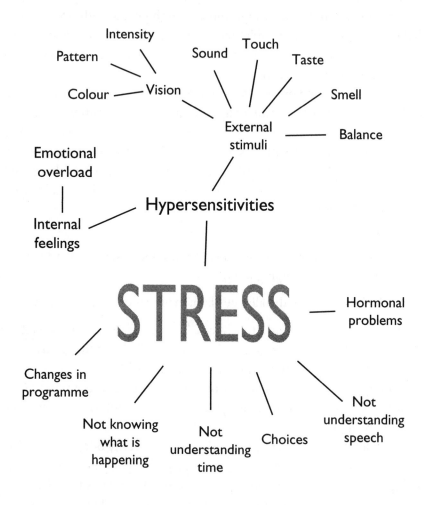

Figure 3.1 Causes of stress

Apart from subdivisions of the familiar vision, hearing, touch, smell and taste there are also sensations attributable to internal and visceral receptors – for example, to the physical feelings of heat and capillary dilation experienced when we are embarrassed. In people with ASD it is not the receiving part of the organ – for example, the lens in the eye – that is faulty, but the processing of the information it has received. A person who is blind may have ASD, but her visual disability is not the cause of the autism.

Of all the senses we know most about vision, partly as the result of work with coloured Irlen lenses which were originally used successfully to treat some people who have dyslexia.

Vision

I am told that a man who kicks the walls as he walks along the passage is 'naughty'. I object to the word 'naughty' instinctively but this does not help me to know why he does it. How can I get an idea of what is going on in his mind? In order to find out I have to put aside my reality; as Donna Williams says, 'stick my own reality in my back pocket and become an anthropologist, exploring his sensory experience' (Williams 1995).

A clue comes from the small boy in the film *A is for Autism* (Arnall and Peters 1992). He says that his 'first drawing is of street lights'. We might expect to see vertical lines but that he shows us is a maze of jointed, wriggling lines. They seem to be all over the place. If we are to believe his pencil, what he perceives is not what we see. This discrepancy begins to make more sense to me when I visit the Imperial War Museum in Manchester, a dramatic building where some of the walls are deliberately misaligned, off-true, sloping instead of vertical, triggering very peculiar sensations in visual perception. I automatically put out my hand to try and check the mismatch between expectation and sensory experience. Since vision is apparently faulty I use touch to verify what is really happening. Which is exactly why the man kicks the walls. What we see as the horizontal boundary between wall and floor, he sees as confusing, swirling about, on the move. A straight line is not necessarily straight so he needs to reassure himself so that he knows where he is and what is happening. The same understanding needs to be applied to people who shut windows, open doors and rearrange furniture. They need landmarks to tell themselves what is going on in their world, where things are. In an unstable landscape they constantly need to revisit and verify these markers.

A man patrols the dining area of his day centre, licking the walls in three particular places. If this activity is interrupted he becomes terribly disturbed and attacks any person who is near him. Another man licks every lamppost that we pass. All these people need landmarks to reassure themselves. Behaviour which seems inappropriate in the NT context may be totally logical within the context of autistic perception. Wendy Lawson (2003) tells us that people with autism 'experience life in a way that enables them to focus but in a way that others do not fully understand'.

A boy in the film *A is for Autism* (Arnall and Peters 1992) complains that his eyes play tricks on him. Quite what proportion of people with ASD experience this particular visual difficulty is not clear. Ann Wright, a teacher who runs the Irlen Centre in the UK (which was originally set up in the US to help people with dyslexia), believes that what is known as the Irlen Syndrome (which is also known as scotopic sensitivity) is so widespread that we should be screening all people with ASD. It is clear that, for many, their visual scenario is that of a swirling kaleidoscope where the pattern never settles. On the other hand, Donna says that when she puts her coloured glasses on, the whole world goes 'shunt' and she thinks, 'My God, that's what the rest of the world is seeing.' When she takes them off again, 'everything sort of slips away again' (Williams 1995).

It is important to understand that what we are looking at here is a purely physical reaction. It is something we can understand and, in a proportion of people with ASD, correct. (This does lead one on to speculate as to how much of the research that is undertaken with people with autism allows for this factor, since it is easy to misinterpret what amounts to a physical disability as a cognitive deficit.)

Similarly, a non-verbal man who is screwing up his eyes throws away the green glasses which I try on him but looks up and around at the room with amazed attention when I give him red ones, as if he is seeing his world for the first time.

I am grateful to a therapist at a workshop for the following history. When she heard of the effects of coloured lenses she told us that now she understood the behavioural change in a man she had worked with. Aged 33, he has ASD, is non-verbal but makes sounds. When he is anxious he will not sit down, jumps on the spot, repetitively shuts doors and tidies and his sounds become louder. One day he has a fall and breaks his prescription glasses. While these are being mended, support staff give him his sunglasses which have red lenses. There is a significant change in his behaviour, noticed by staff and this man's parents. He is calm and quiet, and looks out on the world with his eyes wide open. In a café he no longer vocalizes loudly and tidies the cups. He now wears his red sunglasses by choice and has been referred for Irlen lens testing.

In some people with Irlen Syndrome, this type of sensitivity can be triggered by intensity of light. A young man with very difficult behaviour lives in a room with the furniture so arranged that the sofa where he sits is opposite the window. When he is sitting up he looks directly into the light and his eyes are screwed up. When he lounges over the end of the sofa, looking away from the window, his face is relaxed. Like the schoolboy who is strapped into a desk situated looking out of the window because his behaviour is unmanageable, both these individuals are hypersensitive to light. Looking at the light causes pain. The first step towards helping them and reducing their 'challenges' is low-tech: move the seating. When the furniture is rearranged the disturbed behaviour moderates.

To return to Christopher, he hides his face behind his hand. I suggest to his father that he try altering the colour of the lighting in his room. It emerges that when Christopher is in green light his whole body language alters. He no longer needs to hide his face but can sit up and look around unshielded, confirming the suspicion that light sensitivity is part of his problem. In green light he finds processing his visual intake easier. Unprocessed material no longer threatens to overload him. He begins to take more interest in the world round him – for example, making sounds when TV programmes interest him.

Here we have a paradox. I am told that a child loves red lights. However, when I look at what she is doing it appears more that she is fixating on them in a kind of riveted fascination. Her behaviour is all over the place. When the light is changed to green, she calms, comes and sits close, and joins in games. What is evident from this is that being fascinated by and focusing exclusively on some object or event is not necessarily the same as enjoying it. Sometimes that attention is riveted by a stimulus that is not always benign.

A similar change in behaviour is corroborated by the work of Diane Pauli at Birmingham University Education Department (Pauli 2003) where the effect on children's behaviour of different lighting suggests a link between colour, how they felt and their consequent ability to interact. For example, she found a marked reduction in repetitive behaviour in green or green/ blue light as opposed to red. Exactly why this should be is not yet clear. However, it appears that in people with Irlen Syndrome, the rate of visual intake is out of sync with the rate at which it can be processed and this can be corrected by the use of coloured lenses. *Although in my experience green lighting is most commonly effective in reducing stressed behaviour, it needs to be emphasized that this is not always so.* One can make the discrepancy worse by using the wrong colour or sometimes even shade. An additional complication is that if green room lighting is the most effective in helping an individual, they will need red glasses, the opposite end of the spectrum (Ann Wright, Irlen Centre, private communication). Christopher's family have had him tested and he has been prescribed red lenses. Commenting on the effect of wearing her own glasses, Donna tells us that it should be emphasized that it cuts down the number of unprocessed images floating around in her head to two or three, although this is still more than NT people have to deal with (Williams 1995).

Staff will often say that a service user has had their eyes tested and their vision is normal. It is important to realize that this type of visual disturbance is not shown up in a normal eye test and needs specialized investigation. Enquiries need to be addressed to the Irlen Centre. In addition, some local opticians are now providing the service on the NHS.

Gunilla Gerland seems to have had problems with depth perception. She says:

> ...my vision is flat, two dimensional. It does not provide me with any special priorities, everything seems to appear with just the same sharpness of image. The world looks like a photograph. (Gerland 1996)

The Canadian paediatrician Meg Megson suggests that one of the end effects of ASD is damage to the retina, in particular to the 'rods', the organs which process green/red light and also depth perception (Megson 2004). If this is so, it is not surprising that people with autism may have difficulties knowing where everything is in relation to themselves and other objects. It goes a long way towards helping us to understand the scrambled world experienced by those people on the autistic spectrum with visual processing problems.

In addition to light intensity, Irlen Syndrome can also be triggered by certain colours and patterns. In practice, it is best to avoid bright colours, particularly red and yellow – and also jazzy patterns. When working with people with ASD I wear muted colours, never patterns.

I am asked to see a child at school who is becoming very disturbed in the sandpit area. By chance I stand behind him in the dinner queue and hear the cook say to the server, 'Don't give him a red or yellow plate. He'll throw his dinner on the floor.' When I go into the sandpit area it is lined with brilliant fluorescent orange tiles, evidently the cause of his distress. The solution is a paintbrush. Again, a man who trashes his room every day becomes calm when the walls are repainted soft pale green with curtains, carpet, bed-linen and upholstery to match. All his so-called challenging behaviour ceases.

On the other hand a mother tells me she bought a bright green fluorescent mat to cheer up her son's bedroom. Every morning he threw it out on the landing and she told him to take it back. After thinking about the visual disturbances described above, she realizes that what she saw as cheerful was causing problems for her son. His sensory perception is different from hers and she has not been listening to what he was saying in the only way he can.

Indications of Irlen Syndrome include screwed-up eyes, a preference for dim light, a particular favourite colour or an aversion to a particular colour, or, rather more vaguely, any behaviour which may possibly be related to light sensitivity – as, for example, a woman who banged her head on black splodges on the carpet, and spat on dark knots on a light pine table, rubbing them carefully to try to erase them. It becomes clear that what, from an NT standpoint, we saw as a cheerful pattern placed an intolerable strain on her processing and she was trying to cut down on the stimuli which were tormenting her.

Particularly when we are supporting a person who has both LD and autism, *we need to listen to exactly what they are saying, either verbally or through their behaviour,* setting aside our expectations of reality and trying to see the world as they experience it. A small child was refusing to have a bath, saying there was a snake in her bath. Looking at it from our experience of reality, it was thought that she was hallucinating until the occupational therapist bent her head down to the level of the child's and saw what she saw, the strip light wriggling in the bath like a snake. The child was making a very literal interpretation of her visual perception.

The difficulties with visual processing are compounded by the more global difficulty of 'putting things together'. Donna says she can 'see the leaf but not the tree' (NBC film). Ros Blackburn says that she sees objects without context (Blackburn 2004). Wendy Lawson (2003) agrees: '…we have an eye for detail but sometimes we fail to connect it with the bigger picture. We process things in bits, piece by piece, one at a time.' Lindsey Weeks says that, for him, 'having ASD is like living with a glitch on the television' (Weeks Undated).

Another visual trick is that size can alter suddenly. Where we see a room always as the same size, for a person with ASD, the dimensions of a large room can shrink without warning. Lack of permanence is also indicated by the small boy in the film *A is for Autism* (Arnall and Peters 1992) who says, 'The more intently I look at something, the more it slithers away, especially if it is interesting.'

Teachers need to remember this when they press a child with ASD to concentrate. The very act of trying to attend can increase the pressure on the processing system and so may be counter-productive. If we need to draw attention to a particular object it is better to leave it in a strategic place such as on the table where they eat, where the person will see it when they are not under pressure to concentrate.

Talking in general about visual hypersensitivity, Gail Gillingham (1995) says, 'we should look for visual tranquillity'.

So many community homes are highly overdecorated with bright contrasting colours and patterning, walls hung with pictures and rows of ornaments on the shelves. Tranquillity is the benchmark we do well to remember, particularly when we are redecorating.

Sound

Gillingham (1995) also tells us, 'We need auditory tranquillity.' We often see people with ASD put their fingers in their ears. Sometimes this just generally indicates, 'Stop the world, I want to get off.' Sometimes it is aimed at reducing specific sensory input.

We have so many witnesses to the disturbing and extremely painful effects of visual and auditory hypersensitivity. On the tape *A Bridge of Voices*

(Weeks Undated), Lindsey Weeks elaborates what it is like to live with auditory hypersensitivity (hyperacusis). In addition to being painful, hypersensitivity to sound can also result in bursts of noise and fluctuations. Voices that are loud can drop away altogether.

> It's like living with a faulty volume control. (Weeks Undated)

> Even my own voice booms at me. It sounds like a thunder of garbled words being thrown back at you. (Seyburt 2002)

> Sometimes the toilet being flushed sounds like an express train going to run you over. (Arnall and Peters 1992)

We need to remind ourselves that this is a situation of mortal danger that can set off the fight/flight defence system. Particular sounds are quite common triggers for outbursts.

A child tells us he hears the first few words in a sentence and then the rest 'sort of slips away'. There is a blank space, nothing. A child at school says that when the words return he has no idea of what the teacher has said in between – so he loses the message and is blamed for being lazy.

A difficulty that I share with a friend who is autistic is that of hearing what a person is saying against a high level of background noise – for example, in a crowded restaurant. She says that it is not just a question of deafness (as it is for me) but for her, when there is ambient noise, the speech is not just faint but scrambled – so it appears that processing is distorted by overloading the system. We who are NT need to reflect on the effects of too much simultaneous input and always aim to reduce sensory stimulus.

The sounds that hurt can be large or small and different frequencies for different people. Temple Grandin (Grandin and Scariano 1986) complains of a foghorn; Gunilla Gerland (1996) of the hiss of a ventilation system. It can be the click of a ballpoint pen or the sound of knives and forks on china. Pranve, the young man who lives beside an airport runway, is especially sensitive to those engines which have a high-pitched whine. From his point of view it is fortunate that Concorde's landings have now stopped but there are others with a similar high frequency. When we are together his head turns to the right and eyes roll up every time a plane comes in to land, about every four minutes. His distress can lead him to aggressive outbursts directed at others.

It can sometimes be difficult to sort out exactly what the person is sensitive to. A speech therapist told me of a woman who was becoming very disturbed – no-one could make out the cause of her outbursts. At first it was thought she had problems with tolerating people, so the number of people in her room at any time was reduced – but her attacks continued. Next it was noticed that her outbursts normally related to when someone came into the room and it was thought change might be the problem – but she was still getting upset. Finally it was realized that the door squeaked when it was opened and that the squeak was hurting her ears. Oiling the hinges resolved the problem.

Hyperacusis is sometimes worse in one ear than the other, in which case cotton wool can be used to plug the affected ear if the individual can tolerate the feel of it. An audiologist (M. Brown – see Resources) measured the frequencies which caused a man with ASD to have outbursts of disturbed behaviour. He made a hearing aid mould, drilled a hole in it and filled the passage with an acoustic material that specifically cut out the frequencies that hurt. There were no more aggressive episodes. Simple as that. And yet we try all sorts of behavioural programmes to modify behaviour which we see as causing management problems.

One of the complicating problems of ASD is that once a message has started passing round the brain, the brain is not good at shutting off. This is known as perseverance. For example, the brain may go on repeating a sound message long after the source of the sound has stopped. A man has breakfast in a crowded noisy room full of disturbed people. After breakfast he goes into his room and beats his head on the wall and bellows for up to ten hours. He attacks anyone who tries to stop him. Bearing in mind that Weeks says he would do anything to stop the pain including beating his head on the wall, I suggest that the disturbed sounds he is hearing first thing at breakfast continue to circulate through his brain all day. When his support staff arrange a quiet breakfast for him he no longer expresses his desperate distress.

Although we cannot yet disentangle all the causes of ASD, it does begin to look as though we should be looking for physical resolution of at least some of its symptoms.

It is important to remember that people with ASD are far more likely to understand what we say if we speak quietly.

One rather odd feature is that when we talk about the ability to process or not process sound and vision, Donna Williams (1995) says that when she is wearing her Irlen lenses she can also hear better. Is this a question of limited ability to attend or are we talking about a finite processing capacity? Or both?

Balance

Quite a number of people with ASD appear to have problems with the balance organ and it is suggested that they are trying to desensitize themselves by spinning round, bouncing on their beds or violent swinging. Sometimes this activity is deemed age-inappropriate and the individual is given a swinging garden lounger instead. This does not give the necessary jerk to be effective and a trampoline is a better option. The other possibility is that when a person is focusing on the 'jerk', it is a very effective way of cutting down on other stimuli which distress them. The jerk takes their attention away from all the outside world stimuli that threaten to overwhelm them.

A child is placed at the end of the row in assembly in case he needs to be taken out. He gets into trouble because he leans to one side and will not stand up straight. The physiotherapist realizes that he has a problem with proprioception. If there is a space beside him he needs to lean over to fill it up. When he is placed in the middle of the line, with no spaces on either side, he is able to stand up straight.

So I say again, in order to understand the apparently odd behaviour of some people with ASD, we have to understand the effects that sensory distortions have on their behaviour. If we make judgements on what we see as 'odd' without looking at their perceptions we shall never be able to help them, because the sensory reality in which they are living is totally different to ours.

Touch

What is it about touch which is so painful? How does it feel? Is it more than the sort of shiver that we who are NT might describe as 'a goose walking over my grave'?

Physical contact gives rise to sensations which range from extreme pleasure to extreme pain. We tend to describe it in terms of arousal, how it

affects us, rather than how it is initiated. One only has to contrast the
'thrill' of a lover's caress with such phrases as 'she makes my flesh crawl', or
'gives me goose pimples', dramatic responses to what may have been a
similar light touch. The point is that the degree of arousal and one's
responses are individual and depend partly on how one views the donor
and partly on how the brain interprets the initial stimulus. It is worth
pointing out that such sensations also arise when one thinks about such
situations as well as when one experiences them, so the need for personal
space can be an extension of the negative arousal difficulties. I am not
going to want to stand close to someone who gives me the feeling I can
only describe as 'making my hair stand on end'.

Sorting out what it is that determines how one perceives touch is complicated enough for an NT. One aspect of negative apprehension of touch
is when privacy and boundaries feel invaded – for example, if the donor is
using the recipient as an object for their own self-gratification as is
sometimes the case with tickling. On the other hand, touch can be a
delight if it is used with the intention of building up communication,
intimacy and trust. How the brain interprets a sensation is critical. If the
recipient has problems with boundaries, as many people on the autistic
spectrum do, then touch may be experienced as massively invasive and
unpleasant.

Hypersensitivity to certain materials may make wearing a particular
garment impossible. Clothes are torn off and thrown through the window.
It is well known that for some people with ASD, light touch is a problem –
they prefer firm touch. Famously, Temple Grandin designed a squeeze
machine to desensitize her skin sensitivity based on the press used to calm
and hold cattle during branding. The degree of skin pain is described as
akin to the electric shock from a cattle prod. Lindsey Weeks asks us to let
him know beforehand if we are going to touch him in order to give him
time for his body to prepare.

As a result of touch, pain may be experienced as dermal or sub-dermal,
as a burning travelling wave. Light touch is also a problem for Gunilla
Gerland. 'To be just lightly touched appeared to make my nervous system
whimper as if the nerve ends were curling up' (Gerland 1996).

Gunilla's skin is so extremely sensitive to touch that she cannot bear to
have a shower. 'The drops of water hurt, they had sharp little points that
hurt me.'

At eight, she could no longer bear to have her hair combed. 'It seemed to burn like synthetic fire all over my head and the nape of my neck. In some remarkable way my actual hair seemed to hurt, a pain that I also felt inside my ears.'

She also experienced pain on the inner side of her teeth – pain that was only alleviated by being able to chew.

Trying to help people understand the pain of touch hypersensitivity, in an address to the American Psychological Society, Temple Grandin said:

> If you put on a pair of scratchy pants and then took them off, that would be the end of your discomfort. But in the same position, I should still be feeling the pain a fortnight later.

This not only speaks of the degree of discomfort but also the inability of the autistic brain to switch off. As with the man described earlier in the section on sound hypersensitivity (p.48) who was still screaming and beating his head ten hours later as a consequence of noises he heard at breakfast, the painful messages go on and on and on being passed round the perseverating brain.

A mother tells me she longs to hug her child but, when she does, her daughter bites her. She agrees when I suggest to her that it is because she loves her child that she wants to show her affection. I tell her about Temple Grandin, who says that as a child she longed to be hugged but when it happened she felt overwhelmed and swallowed by a tidal wave of unpleasant sensation (Grandin and Scariano 1986). This mother may have to love her child so much that she puts aside her own need to show her love, out of respect for her daughter's distorted sensory perception. What is being asked for is a recognition that in order to express the love she feels for her daughter, she has to find a different way of demonstrating this. She has to put the reality of her daughter's sensory experiences over and above her natural maternal instinct to enfold her.

It is worth noting that many people with ASD can tolerate touch on certain parts of the body whereas it is perceived as pain if applied to other parts. This can be critical if one is trying to set up interaction which involves touch. For example, a deaf-blind man, who was unable to hear or see a response and rejected touch violently to his hands and arms, was highly amused when his movements were 'drawn back to him' on the top of his foot. Before we use touch as a way of communication, we need to identify where a person finds touch acceptable.

Touch may be the only way we can get through to some people. As an aid to communication it should always be used with respect. It is important to have a management strategy which all users are obliged to read and sign in order to protect both partners in a communication partnership.

Smell and taste

We know less about hypersensitivity to smell and taste. They are diffuse and less easy to measure. However, we do know that smells and tastes which *we* may like can be sensed as disgusting by someone with ASD. A mother tells me her son became very distressed when she opened the door of a fridge which contained egg sandwiches and was hit by a wave of their smell. A consequence of the problem with taste is that a person may not enjoy their food. But Gunilla tells us that this is not always because of the taste; it can be the consistency (Gerland 1996). Quite a number prefer dry food. Then there is the added complication of synaesthesia.

Synaesthesia

The condition of synaesthesia occurs when there is a cross-over between senses so that one sense is perceived as another. It can happen between any of the senses.

Synaesthesia was first named when a neurobiologist visited a man who complained there were too many triangles in the soup (it was too salty). His friend experienced taste as shape. Synaesthesia is not confined to the autistic population but its distribution in people with ASD seems to be more prevalent than in neurotypicals. In the film *Jam-Jar* (1995), Donna Williams shows her friend Paul some soap and comments that it has a very 'green smell'. (Smell is experienced as colour.) A woman throws her custard on the floor saying, 'Can't eat that, it's too black.' (Taste is experienced as colour.)

A small boy confused 'cold' with 'wet' and for him any cold surface is perceived as wet. Feeling emotion as colour is quite common. Gunilla experienced her internal feelings in this way (Gerland 1996) – 'not under-standing' was pale orange; 'tiredness', when she no longer had the energy to try and understand, she saw as dark green. Her colour code became a way of connecting different experiences, rather like metaphor can be used to connect different experiences which have the same affect (feeling quality). She says that if her mother said something in a 'violet' tone of voice in the kitchen and then later also used the same tone in the bathroom, she could begin to find connections between these two rooms (such as there was water in both), but the first link was always made through colour. When people who do not have it come across synaesthesia, it always feels bizarre, since what we perceive as sensory distortions threaten our sense of reality, what is the case for us and what we know to be true.

What is clear is that the sensory feedback (how people with ASD perceive their environment and their internal sensory feedback, how their body feels) is different to the way we who are NT perceive ours. Each person will have different sensitivities and it is our job to try and work out which stimuli an individual experiences as painful. Desensitization is extremely difficult and not often successful. It is certainly not helpful to shrug off the inputs a person experiences as painful and say they'll just have to get used to it. On the whole they do not because this is how their neural networks are programmed. Even if they appear to get used to a stimulus, this is often at the expense of raising stress level and consequent behaviour problems. Fortunately, even if it is difficult to reduce the frequency with which an individual has to experience the painful sensation, in Chapter 5 on using Intensive Interaction we shall see that it is usually possible to find an alternative approach which diverts the attention away from the painful stimulus, refocusing the brain on an activity that the brain recognizes as having meaning for it. This can be thought of as an external substitute for the inner world landmarks in which the brain takes refuge.

We could apply the words of the poet Gwyneth Lewes, writing in this case about people recovering from a mental illness (Lewes 2003). She uses the metaphor of a ferry coming into harbour, navigating by lights:

> They have to learn to distrust car headlights, that a landing star is a plane. *They need new marks for self-navigation, to know where they are.*

In the case of autism, it is we who are going to have to put the markers and buoys into our world to guide them through the sea of sensory chaos. They are going to have to be ones that are recognizable and significant to the individual brain before it can navigate the tricky channels of our world.

Wendy Lawson (2003) says that it is easy for her to focus her attention on things which interest her and terribly difficult to do so on things which are outside her range of interest. When the brain is fully engaged in this way, it usually manages to ignore the stimuli which are so painful – the processing difficulties appear to melt away when the brain relaxes into its familiar territory, even though attention is now outwardly directed rather than inwardly. Communication with the outside world is now possible.

As well as sensory overload directly derived from the world outside, there is also that which stems from the feedback of internal sensation. This is known as emotional overload.

Emotional overload

It is particularly difficult for us NT people to understand how emotional overload 'feels', what is meant by it. The term itself seems to run counter to what is the popular image of people with ASD – cut off, not showing or feeling emotion.

First, we need to understand why it is that 'people' present a particular problem of overload (with its accompanying fear of fragmentation) for those with ASD. Therese Jolliffe explains to us why this is:

> If you have autism it is very difficult to hold a shape in your mind. If the shape moves, you have to process both the shape and its movement. If the shape makes a noise, then you have to process the shape and the movement and the sound. (Jolliffe *et al.* 1992)

Each sensory impression has to be passed through the bottleneck of processing. If we bear this in mind when we think about people, we see shapes which are constantly changing appearance, moving round and 'making all sorts of demands we don't understand'.

While we who are NT have no problem interpreting multiple sensory input, this is not possible for those who have ASD. A man on the able end of the spectrum says that he looks at people's noses (a relatively neutral point on which to focus) instead of their eyes when listening to them – he cannot manage to interpret both the visual and auditory input simultaneously. This type of deliberate strategy is not available to those with severe learning disability.

This raises the problem of our insistence on making eye contact. Therese speaks of this as unbearably painful (Jolliffe *et al.* 1992) while Donna simply calls it agony (Williams 1999a).

Recently published work using scanners is shedding light on this painful state of affairs which leads people with autism to look away. A pre-liminary report of recent research at the University of Wisconsin-Madison illustrates the reality of the physical difficulties encountered here. MRI (magnetic resonance imaging) brain scans show that, when children with autism who avoid eye contact are shown photographs of direct gaze faces, even familiar ones such as mother, the amygdala is more active than in either NT children or children with learning disability and the child perceives the face as threatening. A hyperactive amygdala causes the child to look away.

Professor Richard Davidson asks us to imagine 'what it is like to walk down the street and interpret every single face as a threat, even those you know' (Davidson *et al.* 2005).

Indeed it is possible that the mother's face presents particular difficul-ties since it carries an emotional charge which those less familiar do not. However, during a session of Intensive Interaction, when Pranve's stress level came down, he went over to his mother, whom he frequently attacks, put his arms round her and embraced her lovingly. When the stress was reduced he no longer perceived emotion as painful.

So in other words, people, just by being people and having faces, can overload the processing system of a person with ASD and thereby pose the threat of fragmentation. We don't even have to do anything bad; we just are a source of overload. Better to cut us out of the equation. On the first page of *Nobody Nowhere*, Donna Williams gives us a very clear description of how she learned to look through them:

> I discovered the air was full of spots. If you looked into nothingness there were spots. People would walk by obstructing my magical view of nothingness. I'd get past them. They'd garble...I'd ignore the garble looking straight through this obstruction, soothed by being lost in spots...even people became no problem...I could look through them until I wasn't there. (Williams 1999a)

One of the overriding consequences of autism is that the brain becomes extremely ingenious at blanking off those parts of the landscape liable to precipitate fragmentation. For example, Ros Blackburn tells us that when she speaks, 'She might as well be lecturing to a row of empty chairs' (Blackburn 2004).

This feels odd. What is missing is the sense of emotional connectedness. As far as she is concerned we remain object rather than subject.

When I start work with people with ASD, I often pick up this sensation of disconnectedness. Gabriel pushes past me. His body language suggests that as far as he is concerned I might as well be a lump of wood. It makes no distinction between myself and a piece of furniture.

There is quite often no antagonism; that would be for a person to express feeling – but I do not exist as a person. The switch off can be complete, as when a boy says, 'I do not know what people are for.'

Yet we have to be very careful about what we read into this, since our interpretations and our behavioural strategies are derived from the way in which **we** *experience sensory reality.*

There are two arguments involved here, which are sometimes confused. The first is: do people with ASD feel, in the sense of having emotions?

Therese Jolliffe (Jolliffe *et al.* 1992) is quite clear about this: 'We do love people and we do feel lonely.' Ros Blackburn (2004) says she does feel angry. But Therese and Ros are, in spite of their autism, able people and can and do articulate their feelings. They know how they feel. What about feeling in those who cannot tell us what sensations they are experiencing?

A schoolboy with very disturbed behaviour lives in three places: home, school and respite centre. He particularly dislikes support staff in one place knowing what he does in another. To this end he regularly manages to post his communication book out of the transport bus window. Not knowing this when I visit him in the respite unit, I ask him if he has any 'Thomas the Tank Engine' posters in his bedroom (which his mother has told me he enjoys at home). He growls with fury and buries his face in his arm. His key worker tells me I shall get hit if I continue to go down this route. But when I look carefully, his face has gone brilliant red, the deepest flush I have ever seen. It occurs to me that his response (dilation of the capillaries and a function of the autonomic nervous system) is that of someone who is hypersensitive to his own feeling of what we should term 'embarrassment'.

Embarrassment is an underrated emotion which actually generates some of our most powerful sensations, so powerful that we can even find it extremely painful to revisit the situations which triggered them. It reminds us of our failure to keep in with 'the group'. In connection with this, a friend at the able end of the spectrum tells me that one of their greatest fears is making social mistakes. For all of us, ASD and NT, when we have misjudged a social situation and cannot laugh it off we feel rejected – or at least in danger of being rejected, a situation which, from the point of view of a biologist, places us in mortal danger. (If we are rejected by our group we have no allies to protect us when danger threatens, so our very existence is put in jeopardy.)

To help students understand the sensations this can conjure, after promising that I will not enquire into the circumstances, I ask them to shut their eyes and think of the most embarrassing event that has ever happened to them and focus on it. Then, suggesting to them that they put aside the circumstances, I lead them to concentrate on exactly how, what and where their physical body feels. They will describe to you all the sensations of autonomic activity – heat, flushing, prickling, heart palpitations, etc. Asking them to imagine these multiplied a hundred-fold as a hypersensitive response, they will squirm, shake their heads and say such things as 'you don't want to go there'.

The second message propagated is that people with ASD do not understand the feelings, or cannot empathize with those of others (Baron-Cohen, Leslie and Frith 1985). However, not all the subjects (20%) who were the basis of this hypothesis failed to show the ability to empathize. It is extremely tempting to generalize from a selective band of high-functioning people with autism and we have to remember that what we are calling ASD has multiple levels.

Working with people on the least able end of the autistic experience makes one deeply aware of their vulnerability to the hypersensitivities. Having repeatedly witnessed the improvement in understanding that accompanies the lowering of stress (muscular and body posture relaxation) leads one to question how often what amounts to physical disability is mistaken for cognitive incapacity. This is particularly important when it comes to research.

It is true that some people with ASD appear to be unable to handle the feedback they get from their own bodies when they feel emotional warmth. It's too painful. For them it seems to be easiest to understand emotional overload in terms of a hypersensitivity to the body's internal feedback which can also be triggered by other people's feelings. Wendy Lawson (2003) makes the distinction that she can be sympathetic if she is told that this is what is appropriate and needed in a given situation; she just doesn't know this automatically (presumably because she has difficulty in reading facial and body language, not surprising if everything is slithering about). But is this because she is over-feeling and unconsciously cutting out of such activities as face reading because it may, through hypersensitivity, trigger fragmentation? Or is it because the rods in her retina are damaged and she is experiencing the effects of Irlen Syndrome?

Donna tells us that people may actually disconnect the brain from the ability to 'feel' a sensation when they are in a situation they find too painful (Williams 1996). In order to be able to share the feelings of others, we have to be able to 'refer back' to them. However, if we have ASD and do this, we may find it difficult to read their faces, or even if we can, we run the risk of triggering overload and fragmentation in ourselves. For some, but not all, this seems to include the secondary effect of sharing other people's feelings. Switch off and you don't have to go there.

A parent tells me that his small boy with ASD is so keyed into how his brother feels that when he wakes his first action is to look and see how his brother is. If his brother is upset that day, he will be upset. In spite of the fact that they are in different classrooms he is inconsolable if he hears his brother cry at school.

Different people respond to the effects of ASD in different ways. What I am asking is whether the inability to read faces is an effect of the physical distractions and confusion caused by the Irlen Syndrome, or is it an unconscious strategy adopted by the body to avoid situations which are potentially going to cause pain? Or both?

This ability to disconnect (unconsciously) sounds strange to us. Perhaps it is rather like putting a car in neutral: no matter how hard you press the accelerator there is no movement. Quite how this disconnection happens is not clear but that it does happen is evident. Donna describes how, 'in order to be able to process at least something, for two years [she] cut out either "seeing" or "feeling"' (Williams 1996).

She could either see her hand but not feel it, or feel it but not see it, so she never got the feeling that her hand was connected to her body. It was just a thing which floated in front of her and she tried to get rid of it by shaking it off.

Some people with ASD are able to switch off hunger, pain and possibly the diurnal rhythm. Melatonin, which we use to correct jet-lag, helps a proportion of those who have lost their sleep rhythm.

The clearest evidence of this ability to cut out part of their landscape is demonstrated by pairs of pictures drawn by children, without and with their coloured lenses, very kindly shown me by Ann Wright of the Irlen Centre.

A boy is asked to draw what he sees in a room. Without his glasses he draws a bunch of flowers. When he puts his glasses on, the bunch of flowers turns out to be a stencil on the back of a toilet. He draws the entire contents of the room, toilet, bath with taps, door with handle and medicine cabinet with bottles with their tops on. Without his lenses he knew if he wanted to visit the toilet he had to put his knee near the bunch of flowers. In order to at least be able to process some things – or, as Lindsey Weeks (Weeks Undated) puts it, 'to maintain coherence' – the brain is literally capable of wiping out all but one object.

We need to consider the implications of this for teaching situations very seriously. For example, how much is a child in a story circle actually seeing? If they find a group situation intimidating they may well have retreated into their closed inner world and perhaps see nothing but the teacher's watch? Not surprisingly they pay no attention to the group activity.

It is not only *their own emotions* that can trigger the switch off. Robert Hughes believes his son is over-sensitive (Hughes 2003). He says of Walker, 'the one quality he has in such abundance that it almost seems to define him is empathy. He knows his family's hidden feelings no matter how well they mask them.'

On the other hand, direct praise causes him to blush, curl up and hide his face: 'ordinary shyness taken to the hundredth power'. Hughes continues: 'Much of the time Walker's "autism" seems like a strategy which he has devised to protect himself from the emotion he senses all too keenly about him.'

In such people as Walker, it seems as though the strength of this internal feedback is *so* powerful that what we experience as a 'normal emotion' is interpreted by the body as signalling danger and triggering the fight/flight response.

Since the right half of the brain is generally considered to be connected to emotion (as the left half is to logical thinking), is it possible that the hypersensitivity to bodily emotional sensations observed is related to the increased activity detected by fMRI (functional MRI) scanners in the right cerebral hemisphere of people with ASD, as compared with NT people (Koshina 2004)?

Under these circumstances the person may become aggressive (fight) or disconnect from their feeling (flight). Any event that includes emotional warmth is perceived as a threat. This can include eye contact, smiles, praise, direct speech and even using someone's name.

Working successfully with people who are experiencing emotional overload is extremely counter-intuitive. Almost every approach that we see as friendly can be perceived as a danger signal by someone with this problem. In order to avoid pain, the brain can blank off, so that they can appear to have no emotional responses. *But the problem may be* **more** *sensation than the individual can bear, not that they do not feel, so the brain learns to switch off.* One outcome can be that there is a delay between the trigger sensation (which the brain responds to by burying) and the flood of feeling that sweeps over them later on. Such people may have outbursts that appear 'out of the blue'. Support staff are left wondering what on earth has gone wrong since there is no apparent trigger. ABC charts are of little relevance under these circumstances, because there is no apparent link between the outburst and immediate circumstance.

Donna Williams talks about emotional overload in her book, *Autism – An Inside-Out Approach* (Williams 1996). She tells us that in this situation, 'the strength of the sensation is such that the individual feels as if they are being attacked – and therefore responds as if this is so'.

To make connection with those people with ASD who have this problem, we have to learn to intervene in such ways that do not trigger this tidal wave of threatening feeling. For example, if I work with someone who is avoiding eye contact, I deliberately look over their shoulder in order to send a message to them which reads, 'I am not going to do something which causes you pain.' When people say to Donna 'Don't you find it unfriendly and cold if people don't look at you when they speak to you?' she replies that, on the contrary, '[she is] just so grateful that they respect [her] difficulties' (NBC film).

The outcome of such practice can be remarkable. A woman who avoids eye contact, constantly attacks people and is known particularly to dislike strangers comes and puts her arms round me and lays her head on my lap when I look out of the window and use indirect speech when I speak to her.

Another possibility with more able people is to use indirect speech or a computer to talk to them. It takes away the eyeball-to-eyeball connection which they find so intimidating.

If we so persist in a practice such as eye contact which we know is painful, with someone who is trying to avoid ours, it is almost a form of abuse. To look at them and insist they look at you is to hurt them. The effect is as unacceptable as if we were to hit them.

On the other hand it is possible to facilitate the eye contact so that we can look at each other. As we shall see when we start using Intensive Inter-action, once the person relaxes they are able to give prolonged eye contact on their terms. When stress levels are lowered, gaze no longer threatens to overwhelm them.

We are so used to the idea of encouraging each other with praise that we all, particularly teachers, find it hard to understand that it can be counter-productive. After a particularly interactive afternoon a man got into his taxi with his support worker. She began to praise him and say how well he had done. Normally this man would have run away but in the confines of the taxi there was no escape. In a desperate effort to stem her flow he attacked and seriously injured her. He simply could not bear the feedback that was released in his body, from what we would experience as a pleasant and rewarding exchange. Where we know this is a problem we have to value the person as they are and respect the way they experience their social surroundings and our interventions. Wrong-headed though it may seem to us, for people who experience emotional overload we need to avoid praise and any form of emotional warmth.

If we do manage to do this we are often surprised by the warmth of their response. Once they know that we understand the rules of their world, people who are experiencing emotional overload usually open out with unexpected joy. My experience is that people with ASD *do* want to interact if we can find ways of doing it which show them clearly we can do it together on their terms. How we can achieve this will be addressed in Chapter 5 on Intensive Interaction.

Sensory overload (bearing in its arms the threat of fragmentation) can also be triggered by not being able to work out what is happening – probably an outcome of failure to extract meaning from sensory input.

Not knowing what is happening

Donna Williams tells us how difficult she finds it to know what is going on, yesterday, tomorrow and even in five minutes (Williams 1995). Therese Jolliffe says she spends her whole life trying to sort out the pattern of what is happening. It affects her whole life (Jolliffe *et al.* 1992).

We can see that if our visual and auditory worlds are scrambled, it may be impossible for us to make sense of what is happening unless we can fixate on one object. When Christopher twists the material of his vest into his fingers he is giving himself a particular tactile sensation that is a constant in his world which is otherwise experienced as unintelligible.

As we saw, the boy who drew the bunch of flowers stencilled on the back of the toilet at least knew where to stand when he wanted to use it. When a person fixates, in the swirling mass of sensory impressions, they know what they are doing. They can make at least some sense of what is happening in their environment.

But when a person fixates it is very easy for us to assume that they enjoy the object of their fixation. As I already pointed out, the child who is fascinated by red lights is assumed to 'like' them but her behaviour suggests otherwise. When moved to green light she becomes calm and interactive. From our viewpoint we judge that a man who comes close and stares into our eyes 'enjoys eye contact' – but this staring is different in quality to what we mean by eye contact, which is a reciprocal connection, a means of communication rather than a desperate point of focus. The partner is still being treated as an object rather than subject, something I can hang on to rather than someone I can interact with. We may say that a person who rubs their fingers together 'loves' jigsaws, when what in fact they are doing is focusing on the sensation of fingertip stimulation they obtain when picking up the pieces. They are not interested in the jigsaw as such, only as a means of obtaining the tactile stimulus which keeps them focused. Fixation is self-stimulatory and closed-ended whereas real engagement is open-ended and interactive.

If we cannot make sense of what is going on around us, if we have lost all our landmarks, we feel deeply threatened and retreat 'to a safe corner of the mind where nothing can hurt us'. Not knowing what is happening frequently leads people with ASD to take elaborate measures to try to control their environments. This can lead to the brain making false connections. For example, Gunilla says that in order to make certain that her sister returned from school, she had to make sure the room was arranged in a very specific way, with the newspaper on the table (Gerland 1996). This was how the room had been arranged on the first day her sister returned from school. If the paper was missing, it had to be retrieved and put back otherwise, as far as she was concerned, her sister would not return.

Because her behaviour has become so aggressive, it is difficult to find people who are prepared to work with a young woman at a day centre. Support staff are getting seriously injured. A meeting is called at which everybody who is involved in her day sits down to try to work out what it is that is triggering her outbursts. A pattern gradually emerges that outbursts always occur when, for one reason or another, she loses track of what is happening. Her life is a constant struggle to keep control. When she senses she has lost this control she feels in mortal danger – and responds as if this is so by lashing out. The solution is quite simple. Her support staff make absolutely sure that she always knows what is going to happen. For example, if she is working on a one-to-one basis with a member of staff and someone else comes up and interrupts, *before turning away* to address the newcomer, they explain to her they are going to find out what the other person wants. They ask if this is all right. When she nods, they know that she knows what is going to happen. If she shakes her head, *without turning away* they say to the *other* person who has interrupted, 'We'll talk in a minute.' They give control to her. Furthermore, by ringing her before she leaves home, they make sure that she never arrives at the day centre without knowing what she is going to be doing and who she will be with. Once she knows what is happening her outbursts stop completely.

It is hard for us to understand the implications of not feeling in control of what is going on round about us. It is literally life-threatening, especially if we have low self-esteem as this young woman had. Because she felt totally threatened, she was involved in a life-long struggle to keep coherence, to know what was happening. From 'our world' stance one might object that it was going over the top to give her such a degree of control, that she has to learn to live in the real world. However, as a result of always knowing what is going to happen she is now able to interact without living under threat. She no longer attacks people (Caldwell 2002a).

Our problem is that because we feel safe in our reality we cannot imagine how the same experiences can be so totally hostile to a person with different sensory perception.

In one sense this is because, in our protected world, encountering an event that threatens our very existence is rare. It takes a tidal wave to shake us from our security. We are so lulled by the stability of our own everyday experience that we allow ourselves to get drawn into the position of thinking that if we force-feed people with what we know is the 'real world' surely they will come to see things from our point of view?

It is perfectly true that some of the more able people with ASD may be able to learn to function relatively smoothly in our world by intelligent application of coping strategies, but for some, the stress of always having to interpret what is for them an alien reality is played out in loss of emotional access. Unfortunately, among the less able people with autism, this account is often settled in behavioural disturbance. The outer world is simply a place which is too terrifying with its constant threat of over-stimulation and consequent fragmentation. Remember fear is not just about what is happening now but also what may happen in the future.

Speech, understanding and communication

I am well aware that this is the territory of the speech therapist and have no wish to trespass on their terrain. However, there are some general observations that I should like to address which are relevant to how we approach the questions of understanding and communication. We need to remember that communication is two-way – the problem is not just that our partners cannot interact with us but also that we cannot communicate with them.

If we suppose I have become cut off from the world round me, it would be reasonable for me to ask: 'What is communication for? Can't I just exist on my own? Do I need to be interdependent, especially when doing so causes me such distress?' Of course people with severe learning disabilities are not going to frame such questions themselves but in asking them I want to highlight the underlying assumption – that is, that we are creatures who need to communicate with each other and we are interdependent. I need to be able to tell you about my needs and how I feel and I need to be able to get responses from you, to see that you care and, in a biological sense, will be my ally. Also I need to show you I will do the same for you. Perhaps most important of all, to live a rich life, we need to be able to enjoy each other.

Functional language and emotional access

Mostly we think of communication as transferring information, through speech, sign or gesture. But there is another aspect of interaction which is equally, if not more, important to our well-being and that is letting each other know how we feel. We do this through our body language and, although we may not be aware of it, we are constantly monitoring the body language of others. *How* we and others say things is just as important as *what* we say. We look at their eyes, mouth and general body stance to judge whether or not they really mean what they say or whether, perhaps, they are just saying things to string us along. We listen to the way people say things as much as what they say.

To express this type of perception we talk about 'being in touch', 'losing touch', 'in tune with each other', 'getting close', or as Larry O'Brian (2004) said, 'I like people who are in rhythm with me.'

These are very physical expressions of sensory awareness describing the people who we feel comfortable with, who we feel are allies. They are about how we feel and not about what we think of someone. Hewett (2005) puts it nicely when he says that, as far as communication is concerned, 'speech is the icing on the cake'.

The difference between what one might call 'functional communication' (that is, letting you know what I want) and emotional access (telling you how I feel) was highlighted in a discussion with the sister of a young woman with cerebral palsy who signifies her needs by eye-pointing, left for 'yes' and right for 'no'. By going through a long list it is possible for her supporters to work out which tape she wants to listen to. But, as her sister says, it does not enable her to say, 'I feel really pleased and excited about doing this', whatever it is, or 'I am absolutely miserable today, leave me alone', all the bits that express how we feel.

For we are not automata. How we feel is the colourful part of our lives. It tells us not just *that* we are but *who* we are.

Communicating with others is not just functional language which, for example, lets us know if a person wants a cup of tea; it should also give us emotional access as to how they feel and lets them know how we feel. Functional language is like looking through a window and seeing what a person's needs are, whereas emotional access opens the door and lets us in to who we and they really are – it allows us to be with each other. But because of their extreme sensitivity to emotional feedback, when we are working with people with ASD, it is imperative that we look for and find doorways that are non-threatening, that do not trigger painful feedback from the body.

Body language gives us a person's intent. We need to become expert body-watchers. It may be the only way we have of knowing what is going on for people with ASD and how we can get through to them.

We have to go back to Donna Williams, who has taught us so much about the conflict between the inside and outside worlds of a person with ASD, to understand why it is that speech can be such a difficulty.

In the film *Jam-Jar* (1995), Donna illustrates her thinking process by using model plastic cows as people, one of which is weighed down by a lump of blue-tack. This is the person with ASD and she says she is a bit wobbly. She tells us that her 'way of thinking' is to build up what, speaking as an NT, I can only define as a 'encyclopaedia of sensations without inter-pretation'. 'The table is a flat square, brown, thud thing' but she cannot go from there to name it 'table', nor to put it in context, as in 'the table is the place you put the plates on'.

At the same time, we have to remember that Donna is a highly intelli-gent woman who speaks four languages. Ros Blackburn (2004), who has the superb linguistic skills of a savant – what she rather more interestingly calls a 'speak-freak' – also finds it impossible to place objects in their relevant context. She describes it as like looking at the world through a cardboard tube. You can see the light switch but not be able to relate it to: 'This is the light switch which will switch on the kitchen light.'

Donna says that the constant strain of being asked to live in a world where the most basic organization of our language is related to context and interpretation (and being shouted at for being stupid) set up a war in her head. It was easier to retreat into her inner world where there was no rejection (Williams 1995).

This brings us to one of the central dilemmas of getting in touch with people with ASD, particularly the less able. We are so desperate to bring them into our world that our efforts to frog-march them into sign-systems, or speak *our* language, may in themselves be driving them back into their inner world – it is less painful than trying to make sense of what Donna calls the 'Blah-Blah' out there. Quite simply, we are adding to the stress that a person experiences. Stress level is at the core of whether or not a person can process their intake or not. *Quite simply, the more stressed a person becomes, the harder it is for them to sort out their sensory intake.* If we can find ways to reduce the stress they are experiencing, then the brain works more effectively. We can watch this process in the training video *Learning the Language* (Caldwell 2002b). As Gabriel's face and body language relax, he starts to introduce new ways of communicating and is able to refer back to me, initiating deep eye contact.

Sometimes, as the person relaxes, they start to be able to generalize and to understand quite complex sentences with dependent clauses. A woman who is totally absorbed in her own world, and only responds to speech with aggression, is intrigued when I twist my hair as she does. Using indirect speech and avoiding eye contact I say, 'If I had been doing this for some time, I should want to brush my hair – and if I wanted to brush my hair I should put my hairbrush on the bed.' She immediately bangs her brush onto the quilt. When I walk over and brush her hair, still not talking directly, she leans forward and lays her head against my stomach, desperate for contact.

Depending on the severity of the learning disability, we may be surprised when people start to talk. The video of Pranve shows his movement within the space of three hours' work with him, from the use of one repetitive sound to singing a song with good, clear diction (which surprised his speech therapist who had not heard this before).

A young man who spends all his time rocking in the passage making little grunts, and hitting anybody who passes, stops his aggressive behaviour when his team echo his grunts. He can now be taken out to a pub where he will put his money on the counter and say what he wants: 'Coke.'

With some people the ability to use 'our language' in a relevant way is already present and can manifest itself once the level of confusion is reduced.

When we are trying to find ways of getting in touch one of the most important criteria is to ask of every activity we initiate: *'Is what we are doing adding to stress or reducing it?'*

(Just to complicate the situation, there are also times when non-verbal people will produce speech under circumstances of great stress. However, this should not lead us into the belief that 'they can do it if they try' since to act on this assumption and try to force what is known to exist but is not readily available is to invite behavioural disturbance.)

So the very real problem that we face is whether to encourage performance in our world at the expense of increasing stress. Is there a way through this dilemma?

A schoolgirl aged 12, who I have never seen before, is very good on her computer and can write complex sentences, spelling three-syllable words correctly, but she is clearly very stressed indeed. She puts her hands in front of her face and drums her fingers on her nose. When I drum the same rhythm on a cupboard, she gets a bit more agitated and then turns to me and in a very high pitched tiny voice says, 'Why you doing this?'

It sounds as if her whole self is being squeezed through a pinhole in her effort to speak to me in my language. I reply that I am drumming my fingers because I want to chat to her. Her whole posture changes. She comes over to me and takes my head between her hands and looks deeply into my eyes. She then lays her head in my lap, transformed into the loving open child that she is.

The problem here is that she has learned how to communicate with the world outside but doing this is extremely stressful and underlies extensive behavioural problems.

How can we resolve this? Should we be aiming for someone who can speak our language but is very stressed, or someone who has access to their emotional strengths, to whom we can give ourselves and from whom we can receive, someone who we can truly 'be with'? This is what empowers a person, that they feel good about themselves, not always on the run from a sensory jungle which threatens to engulf them. Under these circumstances many of the behavioural problems melt away. Can we find a way that facilitates both emotional access and cognitive processes so that they can enjoy being with us and also understand and cope with their world better?

Hollow words

We are so used to knowing what words 'mean' that we find it difficult to understand that a word, as well as being the bearer of meaning, can also be just a sound. In a sense the word becomes hollow, an empty noise like a jar with nothing in it. This is especially misleading when the people we think we are communicating with can say a particular word, but do not understand its meaning. This often happens with 'time' words, where the problem is not with the ability to articulate the word but that the person does not understand the concept of intervals.

A small boy comes downstairs and speaks to his mother. Their conversation goes like this:

'When's supper?'

'Soon.'

'You know I can't cope with soon!'

'Six minutes.'

'OK.'

And he goes off to wait.

When this child's mother forgets how difficult he finds the abstract words of time, his brain goes into overload, trying to work out a signal which has no boundaries, a meaningless message, tormenting because he cannot decode it. He screams at her. He literally has no concept of an abstract word such as soon, later, etc. Even though he can say it, trying to extract significance from it, how long it means, sends his brain into a whirl of unresolved messages and overloads it. Fortunately in this case, he is able to tell his mother this, and she is sharp enough to pick up on the problem he is experiencing and resolve it for him.

Getting to know each other

When two people meet for the first time we have rituals of introduction, the exact level of which is determined by the formality of the occasion and varies from 'How do you do?' and handshake, to the smile and friendly 'Hi'. We look each other over and make assessments, which if we are honest are based on whether we like the look of the person, fancy them and, in biological terms, feel they will make good allies. In order to facilitate the meeting we try to effect the meeting in such a way as puts the other person at ease. But what puts me at ease may not be the same as puts a person on the autistic spectrum at ease. For example, at a workshop I was asked if I greeted people with a smiling face and open body language. Looking at a video of myself I realized that I did not, for the very good reason that this would be to make a presumption about a person's sensitivities without first paying attention to their sensory profile. (Maybe they are a person for whom eye contact and smiling trigger emotional overload.)

How then should we meet? Imagine yourself in a world where you find it difficult to make out what is happening. Bits of images scuttle about like fallen leaves in an eddying breeze. What happens when I, a stranger, want to meet you? Should I bulldoze straight into your confusion or should I adapt myself to your understanding, waiting and giving you plenty of time to untangle this new invasion of your senses?

A child of three does not interact with strangers. Her fists are clenched and her body turns away. I put out my fist and slowly extend one finger. After a pause she giggles and reaches out with her forefinger. We meet in a way that has meaning for her.

Recently, I came to the house of a woman who looked at me and looked away. I flicked my eyes away and back and we found ourselves in an intimate greeting game. At this stage her support worker said, 'Say hello to Phoebe', but we had already introduced ourselves in a language which we both understood. The bonding was broken as we were jerked back from the introduction which had meaning for her, for both of us.

Introductions are first impressions and if we get these wrong we may set up a pattern of fear in the brain of the person we want to meet. If the person has ASD, we may not get a second chance to unscramble an irreversible blueprint we have laid down.

How can I say hello to Pranve, who is a man with a long history of disturbed behaviour – and who I have been warned may attack me? When his mother opens the door I do not go straight in but listen. He is in another room and is making soft sounds to himself. I want to make contact with him without triggering his fight/flight system so, *before I meet him*, I join in his sounds. He comes out at once to see who it is that is speaking his language, the sounds that have meaning for him. By continuing to reply to his sounds in this way I confirm that I will talk to him in a way he finds non-threatening, since it will not overload his brain. He leads me at once into the sitting room and sits down beside me. We start to interact. At first he sits with his body turned away from mine but within a few minutes he has turned towards me. He is smiling and giving me his hand. What he has already picked up from me is that here is a person who understands his world and will take great care not to do anything which will add to his sensory confusion. He can interact with this person in a way that makes sense to him (and to me). From strangers we have already become communication partners with all the potential of getting to know each other and being friends.

Clarity, gesture, sign and speech

We use far too many words and need to simplify our communications. One of the problems with ASD is that sign may be far too abstract to aid understanding. Struggling to decode it can actually add to stress levels – which makes communication more difficult rather than less. In desperation, some will learn to make the correct sign without having the slightest idea what it means, in the same way they will learn to say a word without knowing its meaning. On the whole I find that combining the simplest possible question or comment with very clear gesture is the most effective way to communicate. I use this particularly when I am working with someone whose behaviour can only be described as dangerous. I want to make absolutely sure that before I undertake something they know what I am going to do.

For example, before I enter the room of someone with ASD who is disturbed, I stand at the threshold and point to myself and into the room as I say, 'May I come in?' I will then wait for a nod of agreement. When this comes I will cross the threshold and stand still. The message I want to convey is that I am not going to do any action which will make it difficult for them to process, with its threat of tipping them into pain. I go through the same ritual if I want to sit down, pointing to myself and the chair and saying, 'May I sit down?' If they shake their heads I wait and try again. As well as a question of safety, it is also one of courtesy. I am going to wait for them to indicate that they know what I am going to do before I do it.

How often do we barge straight into people's rooms? We may knock but do we always give them time to answer (which may be some time if they are having difficulty processing the sound of our knock)? What does our knock sound like to them? We must treat other people's sensory experience as valuable. In valuing what has meaning for them we should not ride roughshod into their world, insisting on a reality which may have significance for us but to which they are unable to relate – and which can have disastrous outcomes for them. If we ignore what has meaning for them, we are telling them that they and their world have no meaning, a very effective way of reducing self-esteem to floor level.

As well as using accurate gestures such as pointing, we also need to think about the content of what we are saying. What does it tell the person we are trying to communicate with? Has it taken into account that even if we have made clear what we want to do with them, we may not have sufficiently anchored this information in a context which feels safe for them?

Wendy Lawson (2003) says that from the point of view of a person with ASD, 'neurotypical people do not finish their sentences'. For example, they say they are going out but do not say they are coming back. The same rules apply if we are using gesture with people who have no speech. We have to find a non-verbal way of giving sufficient information to cover all the contingencies. They need to know the whole story, not just the first bit which leaves them hanging in thin air.

A woman is very distressed and aggressive if asked to go out for a walk. Thinking she has misunderstood, I try using gesture, pointing to her and myself and then the door, saying, 'You and I are going for a walk.'

This does not help and she is still upset until I realize that, for her, a walk is open-ended and therefore 'unsafe', because she may not know that she is coming back to the place she started from, some place where she does feel safe, somewhere she knows where she is. So I point to her and myself and the door and then, pointing back to the ground by her feet, say, 'You and I are going out for a walk and then we are coming back here', and off we go together.

She is now quite happy to go out since she knows where she will return to. Similarly, when we are working together and I have to leave her temporarily, I point to myself, then where I am going – and then back to her to let her know I am returning. In non-verbal terms I have finished my sentence. She waits quietly.

When we are trying to understand a person's difficulties we have to look at the problem from their perspective which, in a confusing sensory world, very often means putting over what we want in such a way as guarantees for them their safe return.

People with ASD are well known to be very literal. We sometimes forget what this actually means. Ros Blackburn (2004) tells us that when the telephone rang and her mother said, 'Can you get [answer] the telephone?', she disconnected the telephone and brought it. She was surprised when her mother was annoyed because Ros had done exactly what she had been asked to do.

Literalness is one aspect of the inflexibility that is so deeply embedded in the autistic brain which spends its whole life, all its energy, wrestling with apparently limitless sensory chaos. In order to survive in a world of constantly shifting goalposts, every single step of the way, every nuance has to be hard-wired in.

We NTs do not see this – our reality does not present us with such problems. We design programmes on the basis of our experience without making allowances for disorder in the functioning of the autistic brain.

A woman is taught to use a washing machine. She receives praise for learning this, which in her case (although this would not be true of people with ASD who experience emotional overload) helps her to feel good about herself. There is considerable investment by support staff in helping her towards independence. They also have achieved a goal.

Unfortunately the message they have actually taught the woman is that when a garment is soiled she must wash it, so she uses the washer non-stop to launder individual socks/pants etc., an unacceptably expensive activity. When support staff try and explain that she should wait until she has a number of garments, she becomes aggressive. What should they do?

The first problem is that this is a case of faulty programming. It fails to take account of the autistic reality where one message, 'I must wash my sock', clashes with an alternative, 'I must not wash my sock now.'

The two conflicting and perseverant messages overload the brain and threaten to tip it into fragmentation. It may be seen as treading on the brake and accelerator at the same time. Abrasion, sparks fly.

The second question we need to address is to ask ourselves, what can be done to remedy a situation which is leading to a breakdown in care? How is it going to be possible to introduce an escape clause into this battle of the opposing messages?

Although not directly involved in this particular situation, on the basis of experience I should suggest an approach along the lines of having a large basket with a label on it, say '6', into which dirty clothes are counted before they go into the machine. In order to help her know what is expected, she needs visual clues to redirect her programme and provide a route out of the conflict.

Theo Peeters (1997) tells us that change is not impossible, simply unexpected change, and that we need to provide visual clues to assist processing. These will have to be designed at a level that the person can understand. For example, if the woman in this story is unable to count, it would be better to provide a row of six hooks for her to hang a garment on each, so she could see when she had enough for a wash.

Our need to be precise when communicating with people with ASD may take the form of having to define what we mean much more clearly and carrying our meaning right through, by gesture if the person does not understand speech. Even with people whose comprehension of our language is good, I quite often find it helpful to reinforce speech with gesture, using my hands and facial language in a way that just becomes part of our communication. We take for granted our common reality and so skip what we take as understood when we talk to each other.

Restricted speech

People who appear echolalic – that is, use repetitive speech patterns – are often availing themselves of the only speech they have as a window to try to express something they want. What they actually say may be completely different from what they want to say, which is very misleading. They may be trying to express a need and all they can get out is their one limited phrase. Sometimes this will be about a childhood trauma. Yet again they may be just simply trying to join in.

A man can only say, 'See Daddy, change clothes, go home.' If people do not understand what he means he becomes aggressive. I shadow him at lunch. He eats his first course. The second course is yogurt. His eyes flick round and then he starts, 'See Daddy...'

His support worker addresses what he is saying (not what he is trying to tell us) and says to him that he is not going home until tomorrow. He starts to get upset – I was going to say 'wind himself up' but this phrase expresses his actions from our point of view. It implies there is a voluntary element in his escalating distress, whereas what is happening is that his brain has fallen into a struggle trying to work his way through the double bind he is in. He knows what is wrong but cannot put it over to us. (In the words of Therese Jolliffe (Jolliffe *et al.* 1992), it is so frustrating when you cannot get people to understand that she wanted to scream and break things and sometimes to hit people.) In this case it is clear that what he is trying to say is that there is no spoon for him to eat his yogurt. I suggest his support worker asks him to fetch a spoon. He calms at once and fetches a spoon, sits down and eats the rest of his meal.

If a person is only able to speak through a narrow window of words, what is needed is very careful observation of their situation. Most of us are not as good at observation as we think we are. We tend to be guided by our expectations and not see what is actually happening. Sometimes this is because we are operating within the straitjacket of a specific programme and sometimes because what we do see just does not coincide with our reality. We need to distinguish between their real need and their expressed need and not get drawn in to what is, in fact, their only way of telling us that they *have* a need. When they start on 'their key phrase' we have to understand they are trying to convey meaning but not necessarily the one that relates to the actual words they are saying. We need to work out from their circumstances what they are trying to convey to us.

Swearing – a passive acceptance approach

I am fully aware that what I am going to say in this section will be considered controversial. Before rejecting it out of hand I would ask you to read the whole of it and reflect on what I am really saying – and whether or not finding a way which appears to help is more important than our normal social conventions and inhibitions.

I want to look at an area of our lives that is extremely sensitive and I do not want to be misunderstood. I am not advocating the use of swearing with people as a general rule. What I am saying is that there are special circumstances when the use of a particular word in the passive sense and respecting how the person feels may be the only way of helping them.

Swearing is quite a common 'management' problem and is seen as such when sometimes the only speech that people do use is what we term 'bad language'. It is surrounded by all sorts of inhibitions and feelings about what is proper behaviour and what we 'ought' or 'ought not' to do, mainly stemming from blueprints laid down in our childhood. Because we may find it shocking and also because people in the community may find it shocking (and it presents a negative picture) we try to stop the people we work with from swearing, an approach that is rarely successful. Even if it works at the time it does not stop the person repeating the objectionable language next time. In many cases, trying to stop people swearing actually promotes it because they are getting what is, for them, a significant response.

And in some ways our attitude to swearing is hypocritical, since the people we work with have learned to swear from our world. Every time they watch TV they hear it. Every time they walk to the supermarket, go into a café, walk down the street, they hear it. Many of us ourselves swear. So we need to examine the conditions under which we try to stop people swearing. If we are honest with ourselves we discover that this prohibition is what we do to children when we are bringing them up. In our world, just as we do not tell adults to say please and thank you (a common enough work practice), although we might express a wish, we rarely tell adults to stop swearing. These are parental practices which become part of our approach because we are so anxious that the people we work with present themselves acceptably. So, underlying this, are we in fact treating the people we work with as we would treat our children?

We need to think why it is we swear. Swearing is a way of expressing something we feel or need. It enables us to express an emotion. It is one of the few ways that people who are isolated can get a reaction that feels meaningful. For a moment we have the attention of others, they are alongside us, even if in a negative way. Searching for a togetherness they rarely feel, momentarily it helps a person who feels powerless to feel powerful.

There are many reasons why we may feel the need to attract attention in this way and it is true that it may become habitual. But it may also be that we have an inside hollowness that is not being filled, the emptiness which accompanies low self-esteem – I am not worth anything as a person. We do not have to look far into the lives of those who have been in institutions or are constantly being made aware of failure to see how this situation arises. And sometimes the only way families can cope with the situations they find themselves in is to continue to contain a growing person as a child. It is often difficult for parents to make the emotional shift that is required, to allow a person to feel adult if they remain totally dependent. Although they may be cognitively impaired, emotionally the adult/child may feel absolutely powerless and angry.

A manager tells me that every morning when he enters the house, a woman leans out of the window and shouts abuse. Other residents laugh, so she is getting attention which she needs from her peers. His question is: should he ignore her socially unacceptable behaviour? When I ask him how long this has been going on he says, 'six months'.

He agrees when I suggest that, in this case, ignoring her behaviour is not proving an effective way of reducing it. I tell him about a young man who was mending a door in my workshop and who had run out on me, shouting that he was not 'going to work with a fat pensioner bitch'.

I sent a message to him saying if he wanted to talk about this he should come back and do so. He came back quietly and nothing was said until it came to going to lunch. He was asked if it would be all right if I came too. At that stage I looked at him firmly and said, 'That is if you can bear to eat lunch with a fat pensioner bitch.'

He roared with laughter. We had found a way of relating to each other, which was a crucial step for him as he had problems with older women.

To go back to the manager, I suggested that he simply accept what was said to him and agree that it was a pity there were things about him that upset his tormentor. Acceptance is almost always successful in taking their 'fun' out of the interaction. From her point of view this is no longer a way of getting a rise out of him.

Each time a person is told not to swear, apart from giving them the rise they are seeking, we turn our backs on the reality of *how they actually feel*. In trying to control the swearing of this man we were ignoring his very real psychological problem with older women, which was underpinning considerable aggressive behavioural problems. I agree with Bernard Emblem (Emblem *et al.* 1998) when he tells us that there are times when ignoring or controlling socially unacceptable behaviour is ineffective. There are times when we need to turn it round by accepting it.

There is a sense in which we need to reach into the disturbed feeling and acknowledge it for the person in a way that empathizes with their plight. This is solidarity, not just 'I know how you are feeling' or the judgemental 'You ought not to be feeling this', but 'I stand with you in your aloneness, I am here with you'.

The next point is illustrated by two histories rolled into one, identical except for the particular profanity chosen. The first involves a colleague who was team leader of a community home at the time. A woman lies on the floor and shouts, 'Piss off.'

This may continue for a long time, which distresses her support staff, but they have not found a way to stop her saying this. When she next swears, her team leader agrees with her and says, 'You sound really pissed off.'

She looks surprised and says, 'Yes, I am', and stops. The person who swore at me used the word 'Fuck'. I went through the same procedure and her answer was the same, a simple 'Yes' that was not part of her normal vocabulary. Instead of swearing to express her frustration and despair, she was able to look at how she really felt and say to herself, 'Yes, this is me, this is how I am.'

When she said 'Yes', she almost sounded surprised as if she was recognizing something in herself she had not seen before. Because of the sensitivity of the issue, I am extremely grateful to her care manager for giving me permission to reproduce the letter she wrote me about using this passive acceptance approach.

> The first time my communication partner told me to 'fuck off' I was very taken aback as the lady in question was practically non-verbal and quite refined and ladylike. I chose to ignore her remark but she began screaming every time I entered her room. Quite a few times she told me to 'fuck off' in her distress. I went through a pantomime with her to try and find out what was wrong to no avail. I felt rather useless and disheartened. I'd tried painkillers but she refused them, food, drinks, nothing would pacify her.
>
> After working on an eight hour shift with her I felt as bad as her and just sat on the bed and told her she had completely worn me out. She told me to fuck off again and screamed. I said, 'Okay, I'm going. I'm as fucked off as you.' She stopped screaming, looked at me and laughed. I asked was she really fucked off and she said, 'Yes.' The shift was a lot calmer after that.

Because swearing is such an emotive subject, I need to emphasize that we are not under any circumstances swearing **at** *the people we are working with.*

The manager continues:

> Although I don't usually swear at service users and I was appalled at myself for doing it, I reasoned that I had addressed her emotional need in an appropriate manner.

This manager felt guilty. However, in feeling she was being disrespectful she got it wrong, since this misunderstands the nature of what true respect really means. In this case the manager had to take herself beyond the conventions (and the rules) of her reality and truly place herself within her partner's situation, even though it contravened boundaries – a considerable achievement, difficult to do. Her partner, the woman she worked with, was feeling absolutely wretched and expressing it in the only way she could. *Nothing that had been offered addressed this until her brain heard the word which actually had significance for her.* Only then was she able to move forward from her distress.

When we use this passive acceptance approach, what we are doing is lining ourselves up with people, putting ourselves alongside their distress.

With a woman who had rather more severe learning disabilities I took a related but slightly different approach. Her key worker told me that she could not bring herself to use the word 'Fuck' so I tried responding to this by using the sound 'Uck', a sound which carried the same force and intonation. My partner laughed. I made a joke out of it and sang, 'Uck, uck, uck.' She was amused and became more attentive to my responses to her movements (since for her this was real interaction which was previously missing in her life) than to seeing what I would do if she swore, which was her way of provoking a response that had meaning for her. In reality, a number of people are swearing because, in a world of scrambled stimuli, it is the only way they can obtain a response that has any meaning at all for them.

In these exchanges people found empathy, a togetherness which reached in to their inner world and touched how they really felt, assuaged their feelings and calmed them – but also helped them to know who they are. This passive acceptance approach has the potential for raising their self-esteem, something which is very deficient in their lives. Someone is at last taking note of how I really feel.

While the approach offered may be unconventional, by taking a passive and respectful stance, we acknowledge the person's feelings. In no case has its use increased the volume of offensive language. On the contrary, there is normally a reduction in usage as the person finds other, more meaningful ways to interact.

Unfortunately, in order for this approach to be successful, it appears to be essential to use the key word, or some verbal element so alike that any difference is unnoticeable. Sympathy ('you must be feeling really miserable') does not seem to be enough. The reason for this is almost certainly embedded in the infant–mother paradigm, which will be discussed in more detail in Chapter 5 on Intensive Interaction. Simply put, the infant makes an utterance, the mother confirms it and this releases the baby's brain to move on. The mother's confirmation of a very specific action or sound is the key factor in a process which we have all been through. It is part of our primary learning process. This is not to suggest the people we work with are children, rather that we all retain the structure of a particular process. At our deepest level, what we need when we are hurt is for our mothers, or mother figure, to reassure and confirm us – comforting our raw distress. She is our first ally and, in this world, we need allies in order to survive. As she confirms us we are released from the repetitive message.

This passive/respectful approach is a remarkably effective way of decreasing swearing and values how the individual is feeling instead of trying to control them. Some support staff may find it difficult to implement because of the very strong inhibitory blueprints that are imprinted in society about swearing. It is sometimes possible to bypass these by discussing with staff very carefully the hurt underlying a person's need to use swear words. While this approach reduces its incidence and sometimes eliminates the problem, it obviously requires agreement from line managers. It is certainly worth trying since it works in many cases where other approaches do not.

Delayed echolalia

When she is upset a woman will hold herself, rock and, for an hour or so, say, 'It's all right to hold the childer, it's all right to hold the childer.'

I try echoing her words back to her without effect, then recall a piece of NBC film introduced by Donna Williams where the teacher is saying to a child, 'Good boy, you've got your pinny on.'

The child echoes back not the words but the music of the words, with exactly the tempo/rhythm/pitch. I try this with the woman I am working with and she stops at once, leans forward and places her arms round me. When I was using words they confused her but when I echoed the sound of the phrase without words, she recognized it at once. Now she could process the music and rhythm of the simplified message and it had meaning for her. She could relate to what her brain recognized.

Recently, scientists have been able to use scanners to pinpoint which parts of the brain are active during a specific activity. Recent research suggests that there is a difference between the way in which people with ASD and neurotypicals respond to speech. In the NT brain the superior temporal sulcus fires when it recognizes speech – but not in the autistic brain, which however does respond normally to non-vocal sounds (Gervais *et al.* 2004). Considering non-verbal people, whose ASD is linked to severe learning disabilities, it would be very interesting to repeat the investigations making a comparison of responses to the sounds which a person with ASD uses to talk to themselves (which are their 'words') and other vocal sounds. Do these initiate the same sort of response as linguistic sounds in a verbal person?

However we communicate, we cannot do so unless we use the form of language to which our partner is most likely to respond.

Time

Before we learn to tell the time, events just happen and we have no control over them. The difficulty with time is that it is abstract. We cannot see it. Particularly there is a problem for people with ASD with understanding interval, a problem that makes organization and knowing what is happening almost impossible. Even if, like Wendy Lawson (2003), they can tell the time, they are thrown by any idea of how much time has elapsed – and the idea of what timing is all about.

We saw how difficult the abstract idea of time was for the child who shouted at his mother that he could not cope with 'soon'. Although we have learned to measure it, time is intangible; we cannot see it. Many people with ASD and throughout the spectrum of learning disabilities have difficulties understanding the difference between 'now' and 'not now' and the length of intervals, and also sequences. It is fairly easy to spot where these are a problem when an individual endlessly asks such questions as, 'When's Joe coming?', Who's on today?'

Answering by saying 'Jo's coming on Tuesday' will only lead to the repeated response, 'Yes, Jo's coming on Tuesday, when's Jo coming?'

In order to address these problems we have to devise ways of making an abstract problem concrete. This means using timetables and timepieces. The design of these is critical. For example, it is no use using photographs if the person has ground/object discrimination difficulties (they cannot pick out the important bits from the background). Depending on the level of their understanding, instead of pictures we may need to use relevant objects with them. These aids must be presented in a form which this particular person understands.

Quite often the problems people experience revolve around the critical business of transport, knowing when they go home. In order to try and help themselves, people with ASD will very often relate one activity to another in sequence, without understanding they are separated by time. For example, they may know that the bus will come after they have had lunch but have no idea that this involves waiting for an interval of two or three hours. After their meal they go off and collect their coats and stand resolutely by the door waiting for the bus to appear, gradually becoming more distressed as it does not, a distress which may lead them in their agitation to become aggressive to others. They know they must pay attention or they may miss the bus with all the disastrous consequences, so anyone who comes near and presents a distraction gets hit.

It is, however, quite easy to make a 'clock', so designed that it presents the interval in a way they can understand. All that is needed is the electric pack which is now the standard inside works of a clock. This is obtainable from a watchmaker. It has a spoke out of the front for the hands. One hole is drilled in the centre of the clock face, which can be made from a piece of thin ply, painted white. We then throw away one of the hands, since it is having two hands which makes learning to tell the time difficult. If we want an hour clock, we throw away the hour hand. If we want a 12-hour clock, we throw away the minute hand. The face should be simple, without numbers. Initially I start with one picture with a line drawn to the centre. We can use white velcro to add other pictures (not black velcro as this is visually distracting) when the person is able to understand the principle involved. (See Figure 3.2.)

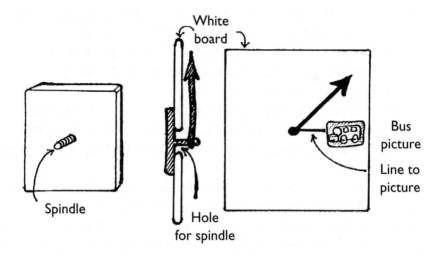

Figure 3.2 Making a simple one-handed clock

Alternatively, we may find it helpful to use timetables. A woman gets off the bus in the morning saying, 'Is that the bus coming?', a question she continues to ask almost non-stop throughout the day. She will attack people if she thinks she hears the bus and can't get to it. I make her a timetable board with a velcro strip along the top. The flash cards are reversible, with a picture of her activity on the front and a plain dark Fablon-covered back. Using velcro tabs on both sides of the cards, it is now possible to turn over an activity as soon as she has completed it and turn up the next activity. In this way she always knows what she is doing at any particular time. She can make a visual check when she is in doubt.

Timers can be helpful with some people to help them understand the difference between 'now' and 'not now'. A woman has been to a school where the day is very structured and she always knew what she was doing. She comes to a centre where they feel this is not adult and she must learn to make choices. She is totally unable to cope with this freedom of choice, since she is unable to process the avalanche of stimuli which it presents for her brain to process. It is simply chaos as far as she is concerned. Retreating from this, she sits naked on the top of a cupboard on top of a blanket on top of a pile of faeces. In her confusion, when she does this she knows what she is doing. She will not come out of the room unless she is made to but when this happens she becomes very upset and screams to go back. I use a kitchen timer to lengthen the time she will stay out. Her brain now has something to focus on, tick-tick is 'not now' and ping is 'now', instead of the panicky struggle going on in her brain previously. She gets the idea very quickly, after using it twice.

Another very simple approach is to use bum-bags to hold a flash card or object relating to whatever it is that the person is currently meant to be doing, so that they have a marker to refer to when they are becoming confused.

A number of schools now use the system called TEACCH (see Resources), either in its pure form or integrating elements of it into normal class work. The basis of this approach is that it reduces the sensory input a child receives by stripping their environment to minimal essentials, cutting down on distractions by using screens around work stations. A child is helped to know what they are supposed to be doing through the use of a panel of sequential reference objects or pictures, depending on their level of understanding – and color coding of the particular activity they are engaged in at the time. For example, a red card indicates doing the activity in the red basket. It also uses timers, so that students can pre-determine and have control of how long they will have 'time-out', a period when they can retreat and catch up doing their own activity. TEACCH provides the simplification and structure which makes it easier for a child with ASD to know what is happening in a school situation. Some flexibility needs to be built in to the leaving transition, otherwise the switch from structure to uncertainty may throw them completely.

Choices and change

One of the golden rules of our world is that 'everyone must learn to make choices'. The problem here is that if you have ASD, both 'change' and 'choice' mean a massive increase in the amount of information which has to be processed. For some but not all people with ASD, this throws an intolerable strain on the processing system. Because they are afraid of being tipped into fragmentation, these people respond as if they are being attacked, with all its behavioural consequences. Again, we have to find ways round this which let a person know what is going to happen in a way they understand. If they are upset when asked to choose, present the choice in a simple way by offering first one alternative and then another if the first is rejected. In this way they only have to process one piece of visual information at a time.

To provide for the difficulties caused by change is more difficult, since the circumstances are very often beyond our control. Wendy Lawson (2003) explains that the minor transitions of daily life can be very traumatic. She says, 'I have to stay here because this is all I know. Outside "here" is chaos, confusion and conflict.' In order to help transition she needs 'order, understanding and calm'.

Theo Peeters (1997) assures us that the problem is not so much change in itself, but unexplained change. As illustrated in the story of the lady who endlessly washed her single garments, a person needs assistance in the form of visual aid, to help them reinterpret what is happening. We need to understand that distress is not just about not being able to do something; it is the uncertainty rather than disappointment that throws the person into turmoil. The conflicting messages 'I must do this' and 'I can't do this' cannot be resolved or exited by a perseverant brain where the messages go on and on being passed round.

To some extent we may be able to provide for unforeseen contingencies if we use a 'jig'. A jig is a detailed sequential plan which allows us to offer escape routes if an unexpected change in events arises. A man is extremely upset by changes in his programme. I make him a board with hooks, which carry pictures of the particular activity that is going to happen next. If his programme is altered, an overlay is placed over the original activity which clearly shows the reason – and an arrow points to an alternative. Now he has visual clues to the solution to his dilemma.

For example, the original picture might be a picture of swimming but on Tuesday the taxi is not available. So the picture of swimming is covered by another picture of a taxi with a flat tyre. This is followed by a picture of the individual and an arrow pointing to a picture of a saucepan, indicating cooking. The graphics used are those with which this man is already familiar from his timetable. In practice we were able to reduce the number of reasons why an activity had to be changed to five. (For example, a picture of a face covered with spots indicated a staff member was ill.) Having graphic support made it easier for him to reinterpret what is an unavoidable change in routine. The extent to which this is possible depends on the level of learning disability. If pictures are not understood we may have to use 'objects of reference', objects which are part of an activity and not signs which are too abstract instead of drawings or photographs.

In Chapter 5 on Intensive Interaction we shall see how putting in familiar landmarks (objects or activities that the brain recognizes) into the unfamiliar terrain of daily life can also assist change, since the individual can focus on familiar landmarks instead of the chaos.

Hormones

Many of the people I am asked to see are boys or young men in puberty. Their behaviour has worsened and those who look after them come to a stage where they find it impossible to draw up management strategies to contain their outbursts. I suspect that the childhood difficulties in processing which are experienced as a result of their particular hypersensitivities become more pronounced during puberty. It appears that the individual becomes much more sensitive. Behaviour may worsen to the point at which it is difficult to get staff to support them.

In *Autism – An Inside-Out Approach*, Donna Williams (1996) tells us that the hormonal surges which accompany puberty are completely out of control. These are described as 'feeling like being overwhelmed with a tidal wave of sensation', extremely unpleasant. The fight/flight system is on a hair-trigger. The person feels as if they are being attacked and may respond as such. There can be similar problems associated with PMT (premenstrual tension) and menopause. But even under these extreme conditions it is often possible to refocus the person's attention by using their individual body language to communicate with them.

Not everyone with ASD will have all the stress problems described above. It is our job to find out how each individual is affected and how we can help them to navigate their sensory chaos.

So far in this book we have looked at aspects of a person's environment or experience and their body feedback which are likely to cause them stress and, as a consequence, make it more difficult for them to process incoming stimuli. I want to go on now to look at the effects of such stressful events and how these contribute to what is somewhat misleadingly known as 'challenging behaviour'.

CHAPTER 4

Behaviour – Challenging or Distressed?

I should like to start this section on what we call challenging behaviour by quoting from Rita Jordon:

> It is rare for a child with autism to display aggression as we normally use the term although they can certainly display difficult and even violent behavior. (Jordon 2001)

I am sure this is also true of the adults that I am asked to see, despite the fact that some of them have managed to acquire the label of being dangerous, which in practical terms means that it is difficult to find people willing to work with them. However, if we bear in mind the stress levels that people with ASD experience, are we right to think and speak about their behavioural difficulties as 'challenging'? Should we not rather think of them as the outcome of distress?

When the term 'challenging behaviour' was initially introduced, it was taken to be behaviour that challenged the service – but so often support staff see it as behaviour specifically directed against themselves. We use expressions such as 'targeting' and very often feel that the person with ASD is the perpetrator of behaviour of which we are the victims. The term in itself sets up an 'us' and 'them' situation which does not help to resolve the stressful and often painful difficulties the individual is experiencing. In reality it is very often they who are the victims of the sensory demands we are placing on them.

Can we have a miracle please?

When I am teaching support staff how to approach working with people with ASD and very disturbed behaviour, what they really want is the wave of a magic wand which will resolve the behaviour they find so difficult to live with. They will produce examples of more and more disturbed behaviour.

'How do you work with a man who drops to the floor and bites your ankles?' is the kind of question I get asked, with the implication, 'bet you can't work with that'. And this is a difficult one but the first thing I ask myself is why this person feels the need to bite ankles. If he has ASD, looking back to coping strategies, I should proceed on the assumption that in sensory terms he is being overloaded. So the next question is: what is it that is causing the overload? Is he communicating his need to get rid of me and so reduce the sensory demand I make simply by my presence? Are there too many people in the room, or is it a particular colour or sound that is upsetting him? Next I need to look at what he is doing when he is not attacking people, when he is on his own. Is there some way he talks to himself, like making sounds (even if these are just heavy breathing) or waving his hand? Can I use these significant signals to join in his brain–body conversation so that we can set up a way of talking to each other which is non-threatening in sensory terms for him, so that he will not need to resort to extremes to get attention that has meaning for him?

'Trading on their autism'

Looking at ASD from our outer-world perspective leads to a complete failure to understand the autistic experience. This was illustrated by the remark made by a teacher to a parent who was trying to explain that her son was not 'naughty' but had real organizational difficulties because of his autism. The teacher said, 'Yes, but don't you think he trades on his autism?'

People with ASD do not trade on their autism; they are far too busy struggling to make some sense of the world about them. This teacher appears to have had absolutely no idea of the distorted sensory reality with which her pupil has to contend. She sees his behaviour only from the point of view of the disruption he initiates in her classroom, an attitude which leads her to lean on him – and his confusion to increase to the point of refusing to go to school. While one may sympathize with his teacher's difficulties, what this particular child needs is support in the organizational aspects of his school day to reduce the stress set up by never knowing what is happening.

Reducing the sensory overload

To go back to the section on coping strategies (p.28), a person with ASD will try to get out of a situation where they are in danger of becoming overloaded by withdrawing and focusing on a repetitive behaviour (which is either based on listening to an element of the familiar landscape of their own body language, or fixating on some object or behaviour drawn from the world outside). If this attempt to focus on their inner world is insufficient, their agitation increases. A man who flaps his hand gently will start to beat it up and down vigorously and perhaps shout. If the source of agitation is not moderated and threatens to overwhelm them, they may well shift their focus from repetitive self-stimulation to the alternative strategy of trying to reduce the overload by removing themselves or getting rid of the source. If a person who is becoming disturbed is trying to get out of the room, it is never a good idea to stand between them and the door since they will be trying to escape the source of the overload and thus avoid being pushed into fragmentation. To present oneself as an obstacle is to risk almost certain attack.

At times the brain will even switch out of processing altogether, so that the person literally does not hear what is said to them. When the brain switches on again, they have absolutely no idea of what has been said. They then become confused and upset because they know a demand has been made but not what it is. We who are NT may assume the individual is just being difficult or lazy, especially as we know that sometimes they can do whatever it is that we require of them. Rather than thinking in terms of challenging behaviour we need to think of the underlying distress the individual is expressing.

When we are faced with behaviour that we cannot manage, there are two questions we need to consider. The most immediate is: what can I do about this now, about Ali who won't come out of his room, John who is screaming, Mary who spits and pulls hair, Sharon who lashes out and Dave who self-injures? Bearing in mind also that, in a person with ASD, these behaviours are almost always a response to sensory overload, have we any strategies to reduce the sensory input or approaches that will divert their attention from the stimuli that they are so sensitive to?

Looking for triggers

In the past we have tended to rely on medication, or containment and restraint, without asking ourselves exactly what it is that is upsetting the person. In particular, the use of restraint with people with ASD is rarely effective since it tends to increase their stress level. Even if it does help temporarily, it does not address their underlying problem, the root of which may be a simple physical hypersensitivity.

First of all we have to understand that if a person with ASD is using behaviour which is becoming upset, it is because they cannot cope with the difficulties the brain is having in processing and the fear that this triggers of impending break-up. We have to remember the force of anticipatory fear. Those of us who may be afraid of flying know that it is not just when we are sitting on the tarmac and the engines are starting to whine that we are afraid but several days before when we wonder if we really want to go on the holiday.

Jolliffe tells us that not only does she spend her whole life trying to make sense of what is happening but that she also lives in terror, not just of what is happening now but that something terrible *may* happen (Jolliffe *et al.* 1992). She is walking on the verge of disaster all the time. Nothing is constant. Even the dimensions of a room can shrink. Mother in a blue dress can be a different person from Mother in a red dress.

Aggression

When Pranve attacks his mother he claws her head. Observation suggests that he is trying to remove the ribbon that she sometimes uses to tie back her hair. He stops when it is on the floor. Just this minor difference in her appearance throws his brain circuitry into chaos and he tries to root out the cause of his confusion. What we have to understand is that, for him, this turmoil is not just some minor irritation but is perceived as life-threatening since it cannot be interpreted and the brain threatens to fragment. The response is part of the fight/flight defence response and fulfils our primary human need to protect ourselves. Pranve's response is the same as if he is being attacked. This is what it feels like for him.

Self-harm

Self-harm is common. If I focus on the pain I will not have to listen to the sounds round me (or those in my head, because even though they are no longer going on round me, the noise keeps circulating through my head). When Weeks says, 'I will do anything to stop it, bang my head on the wall, run in front of a car' (Weeks Undated), he means *anything*. If he focuses on the pain of impact he is trying to divert his brain.

When he is not withdrawn into his inner world of flicking, Gabriel screams and crashes his head on the door. Donna describes how she would run at the wall, like a sparrow beating itself on the window when it tries to escape (Williams 1999b).

Temple Grandin describes the turmoil going on inside the brain as like a lion in her head (NBC film). This is where the individual's attention is. Have we got a way of shifting this attention to the world outside in a way that is so powerful it will divert their focus away from their distress? We need to look at the whole picture trying to tease out the sensitivities and triggers.

When we come to using Intensive Interaction we shall see that with people with ASD we need a dual approach. We need to look at the whole picture, trying to tease out the sensitivities from the triggers and combining this with learning how to connect with a person through non-threatening signals which form part of their repertoire.

Moving attention away from the inner turmoil

One encounter which I have described in *Person to Person* (Caldwell 1998) particularly brought home to me how we have to enter the world of the people we are trying to get through to, giving all our attention to what it is that is disturbing them and acknowledging it rather than brushing it aside. I am introduced to a large young woman with Asperger's Syndrome and warned that if she starts talking about 'number seven' I have to get out of the way since she becomes extremely agitated and lashes out. I make the mistake of being too upfront with her in a way which experience has taught me to avoid nowadays and introduce myself to her by asking a direct question, 'What are you doing?'

She tells me that she is making meat sandwiches for her supper and then starts to back me into a corner, saying, 'Do you know about the number seven? It's very important and there are number seven buses in town and number fourteen is all right because it is two times seven!'

By this time she is enraged, in full flow and I am trapped – but I hear myself say, 'Are you going to have seven sandwiches for supper?'

At this she breaks off, laughs and says, 'No, I am going to have three.' And she returns to making her sandwiches.

We need to understand what has happened here. More by good luck than good judgement, relocating the focus of her attention – the 'number seven' – back into the outer world – 'making sandwiches' – has directed her attention away from the tantrum that was unfolding in her brain. When using this technique, it is vital to go straight for the crux of the message. In this case it was the word 'seven', which she actually tells me is important. As with swearing, discussed in Chapter 3 (p.75), in order to carry off this technique successfully it is essential to use this pivotal word. Sympathy and empathy are not enough. (I suspect that when a person has a tantrum, the brain is stuck with an overriding obsessional message which goes round and round endlessly. It simply cannot move on. The individual reverts to the infantile stage and requires the mother substitute to confirm the particular focus of their distress before they can move away.)

Where there is a recognizable build-up to outbursts this is a surprisingly effective intervention technique which has been used with a number of people. First of all we need to isolate what *is* the critical word that they get stuck on and, since the outcome of this type of tantrum is often violence, work out a strategy for diversion, since one cannot always rely on intuition to provide the critical exit strategy at the right time. How can we reset the person from their inner tantrum to the world outside them? We have to use the critical word as a point-switch to direct their attention down an alternative line.

Sometimes all that is needed is a single redirection. A man trashes his room regularly. No behavioural interventions have stopped this behaviour. His key worker decides to join in and picks up something and drops it deliberately, saying, 'You missed breaking this one.'

The man is surprised. He looks at him and says, 'Oh, you break things too?'

Why does he never trash his room again? It is difficult to say. But the common feature in all these stories is that the person's attention is redirected from a 'stuck' message in the inner world and a link is formed instead with the benign outside circumstances.

Diversion

Behavioural management is rarely simple. It usually involves a cluster of interlinking problems, all of which need to be addressed. Especially when a person has ASD, there are likely to be a number of different sources of stress.

A young man screams and bites himself. His support staff have not found any way of stopping his noises, which can dominate the day centre. The only quiet time is when he retreats to a corner and immerses himself in a catalogue and listens to his record. If this is interrupted he starts his distressed bellowing. This occurs particularly before lunch. We look at a videotape of his behaviour to try and work out what is happening.

1. When he is not listening to his tape, his screams are renewed every time he hears another loud cry or sound. (He is hypersensitive to sound. Most of the time he switches off to these by burying his attention in his catalogue and music so that he can switch off those particular sounds which disturb and hurt him.)

2. He dislikes the music of another service user and she dislikes his. (When he listens to 'his tape' he knows what he is doing and they help him to cut out the sounds and stimuli he cannot cope with.)

3. A bus arrives 20 minutes before lunch. As soon as he sees the bus, he knows that lunch will follow. This is the clue – but he doesn't understand that lunch is not going to arrive instantly, that he must wait. There are two opposing messages which throw his mind into turmoil, 'that it is lunch time' and that 'lunch has not arrived'. His distressed noises set off other service users and the resultant noise is cumulative. (He has a problem with time, which is abstract. He can't see it and especially cannot grasp the idea of waiting.)

I try two different ways of shifting his attention. At first when he screams, I place my hand, gently but firmly, on his shoulder to replicate the tension (he is actually shaking with the effort) in his throat and neck muscles when he is screaming. When he stops, I take my hand off. He looks up briefly but the interaction is not strong enough to shift his attention permanently. (Although this approach has previously been effective with others, it is not so with him.) So I try placing my hand in my own mouth and bellowing when he does, loud enough for him to hear (but a bit more softly). The first thing that happens is that he looks up at me. When he next screams, his voice is lower and he looks out again from his inner world to his key worker who offers him a book. I respond with a lower level scream. After the third response to his scream his attention has shifted completely and is now rooted in the world outside. We have broken into the repetitive cycle going on in his brain. From now on, if he looks up I make a low growling sound in my throat to try to offer him a way of communication through non-verbal sounds which are not screams. (This technique is an adaptation of Intensive Interaction, which is the subject of the next chapter.)

At the same time we need to look at what other practical steps can be taken to help this young man reduce the triggers of the distress he is experiencing. Starting in reverse order with the problem of waiting for lunch, support staff are encouraged to take him for a walk before the bus comes in and not bring him back until his lunch is on the table. This very simple practical strategy removes the time/interval problem and hence the noise at lunch problem. Second, there is the difficulty of mutual dislike of another service user's music. He will not tolerate headphones but the other user will, so they no longer have to listen to music that disturbs them. He can focus his attention on his nursery rhymes, which, while they may be age-inappropriate, help him to know what is happening. His brain recognizes these and he can lock on them to the exclusion of the sounds which hurt him. Finally I show his key worker how to enter into the activities which have meaning for this man. He likes dogs and when he sees pictures of them he laughs and taps his leg. I show his key worker how to join in with this body language so that they can share the things which have meaning for him.

The majority of what is known as challenging behaviour is triggered when people are upset because they are getting overloaded by their environment and can no longer process the sounds and images and sensations which are in their brain. The turmoil becomes too painful, because of hypersensitivity to sensory input, not knowing what was happening, too direct an approach and so on. One way and another they are trying to cope or failing to cope with a situation which is overwhelming them and outbursts are the outcome of our failure to understand what it is that is triggering their distress.

Maintenance of successful strategies

If we find a successful intervention we should not stop it just because the person appears to be able to relate and communicate better. It is critical that we continue with this approach. If we stop, they will regress. It is like using someone's language and then sending them to Coventry. This is illustrated in the history of Roger who has been described in *You Don't Know What It's Like* (Caldwell 2000). Staff learned to 'talk' to him using his sounds and his extremely difficult behaviour disappeared. At this point a new team leader decided that there were insufficient problems to warrant continuation of the Intensive Interaction interventions. Within 24 hours of stopping using his language he was back to throwing the chairs and tables about and hitting people. This disastrous behaviour continued until the programme of using his language with him was reinstated. Learning and using a person's individual language with them does not cure the autism; it modifies their environment, putting landmarks into the outer world which the brain can identify.

Epilepsy

Occasionally disturbed behaviour is related to temporal lobe epilepsy. In such cases the onset is usually extremely rapid and, at the end, the individual comes out of it swiftly. The problem here is that, although sometimes there is a history of epilepsy, it can occur when no seizures are evident and small absences have been overlooked or are not even noticeable. If there is completely unrelated violent behaviour which cannot be tied to any cause it is worth investigating to see if there is any epileptic activity in the brain, if only to eliminate this as a cause of the behavioural disturbance (Gedye 1989).

CHAPTER 5

Intensive Interaction

The dynamic of conversations

So far this book has focused on the sensory difficulties, often extreme, which are the day-to-day experience of people with ASD, the difficulties they have interpreting these and the various strategies they employ in order to survive what is for them a hostile environment. Now we are going to turn our attention to a way of engaging with people who are having such a rough sensory ride, so that we can truly become communication partners. Intensive Interaction is a successful way of reaching out to people with communication difficulties regardless of age, gender and ethnicity.

Whether or not we are aware of it, our brains are constantly involved in a state of dynamic bargaining between internal brain–body conversation and bodily sensations derived from environmental stimuli. We are in dialogue all the time.

Inside there is the Thinker talking to the self, unconsciously and consciously, brain within brain, initiating, reflecting on, matching and shuffling needs and ideas.

The Negotiator's brain talks to the brain of another person, the 'other', exchanging ideas and information.

Then there is the Works Manager, who is involved in the two-way traffic 'brain–body language', sending cognitive brain messages to the body and receiving bodily feedback (in the form of sensation) back to the brain. Basically, the brain says 'Do this' to the body and the body tells the brain 'Done it'.

The 'Playmate' puts aside the analytical pathways in favour of perception. It deals in sensation and shared 'affect'.

What we need to look at is the interplay between our various conversations and what it is that shifts the system in favour of one direction or another. So first we need to look at what happens in so-called normal development.

From infancy, in order to survive we need to identify and pay attention to what is going on round us and decide how it will affect our welfare. We also need to make the transition from listening to self (where the whole world is an extension of 'me') to listening to other. We need to acknowledge and learn about the independent existence of the 'not-me' and define the boundaries between ourselves and the not-me, because we cannot know ourselves unless we have separated from others.

But because of the sensory confusion engendered within people with ASD, the processing system frequently indicates that events from outside are hostile. Safety is sought by retreating into the internal brain–body language, the internal sensory conversations or on fixations. These are the themes which feel safe, activities or behaviours which feed the inner world. In other words, the Works Manager who directs the 'do this/done it' repetitive cycle is in charge and this is where attention is focused. At least here is something which can be relied on not to fragment.

Occasionally contact with the outer world is completely closed down. Partially or totally, the brain turns its attention to objects it regards as part of its repertoire. It becomes conscious of its own internal processes and starts to engage with these in its inner world so that it does not have to take on board the stimuli that so disturb it.

However, to operate efficiently requires flexibility. In autism, because the outside world is perceived as hostile due mainly to the hypersensitivities, the focus tends to harden onto a particular behaviour or, in the case of fixation, an object or activity that is hijacked from the outside world.

But we tend to think a person is not in conversation if they do not engage in dialogue with us. However, a lapel button sent to me sums up the situation succinctly, 'Not being able to speak is not the same as having nothing to say!', and being unable to say what you want and, particularly, how you feel means that the self can become a painful 'I can't get out' repository of unspent affect.

Seeing things differently

A mother who had been watching the video of working with Pranve's sounds objected that what I had been doing sounded to her like 'babble' and that she would have got in early with 'sweets and toy cars and things that kids like'.

This is a vigorous defence of our reality, the way we NT people see things. So why not?

But suppose the child or adult does not experience sensory input (and therefore respond) in the same way as we do. What if the boiled sweet is simply used as a colour filter to look through and twist round, viewing our shared world in a completely different way to that which we do. And the car is a missile whizzing past our ear as the person tries desperately to persuade us to leave as we are endangering their sense of coherence. What if the things we offer mean something totally different to them than they do to us?

Peeters (1997) quotes the story of a man who is asked what he feels when kissed. He replies that it feels 'wet'. In both this and the above story, what the autistic person derives from our input is an aspect of experience that does not coincide with our own. Of course, we neurotypicals know we are right (we always are!) but each of the sensations described is actually being used for the purposes of defence against sensory assault. The transparent boiled sweet colour may be an Irlen filter, a window opening a world that does not slide round, stabilizing the visual field so that all its bits shunt into place. No wonder the child wants to endlessly peer through this outlet into a world that makes sense. The car used as a projectile is the means of simplifying sensory input by reduction, getting rid of the source of the stimulus. The man who latches on to the physical attributes of a kiss, rather than its emotional content, interprets it as 'wetness'. His brain has learned to protect himself against the pain of emotional overload.

Apart from reducing those stimuli which cause confusion and pain in people with ASD, we can also help them by learning their language (the language they use to talk to themselves so that they can focus on this rather than the things that so disturb them). We do this by using an intervention known as Intensive Interaction.

Imitation

There is a considerable body of psychological research which focuses on the use of imitation between mother and developing infant (Butterworth 1991; Kugiumatzakis 1993; Meltzoff and Moore 1995; Nagy and Molnar 2004; Reddy *et al.* 1997; Trevarthen 2001). More recently this has been extended to include studies of children with ASD (Dawson and Galpert 1990; Nadel and Peze 1993). Together these show the positive outcomes of imitative play – increased eye contact and gaze at mother's face, more creative play and longer social interactions.

Significance

The importance of the infant–mother relationship and especially how the mother reflects and confirms the infant messages is primary. This releases the infant to explore a new utterance or movement (and assists them to develop a sense of self). Since I was working with adults my attention was particularly drawn to an exploration of *what it is that has meaning for a person* **now**. Theo Peeters' book *Autism – From Theoretical Understanding to Educational Intervention* (1997) was particularly helpful.

The problem is that if I have ASD, objects and events which have meaning for me are clearly not viewed in the same way by those around me. Donna Williams gives a vivid account of how she was slapped when she spent time 'looking at the spots' in the air which meant so much to her (Williams 1999b). What her mother evidently saw was someone who was switched off and would not attend.

If I have ASD and severe LD, then my inner world objects and behaviours which have significance for me clearly do not resonate in the same way for you who live in the outer world. You see the objects I treasure as a barrier to be dismantled. My sounds and movements are ignored. My fixations are discouraged. What are known as 'stims' (self-stimulatory objects such as a piece of paper to flap) are taken away from me with the intention of forcing me to attend.

As Gail Gillingham points out in her book *Autism – Handle with Care* (1995), this practice has the opposite effect in that it leaves me vulnerable to my hypersensitivities and so raises my stress levels, driving me further back into my own world. If you want to communicate with me it has to be worth my while because all that I have learned so far is that if I make a signal, I do not get an answer that is meaningful for me. This has not been happening – almost all the things you do will be nonsense for me and add to my confusion. I need to know that if I send a message, you will respond in 'my language'. Otherwise I shall give up trying to make contact with you.

A child with ASD may simply be unaware that words are for communicating. When they feel they are becoming over-stimulated they may focus their attention exclusively on an inner world, self-stimulating by listening to some internal bodily rhythm, even one as simple as that of their own breathing or listening to the sound made by sucking their saliva.

Repetitive behaviour and the brain–body language

In the repetitive brain–body conversation, the brain behaves as the works manager organizing what is going on in the body. It sends messages saying to the body 'Do this' which are answered by feedback from the body in the form of sensation saying 'Done it'. If the brain fails to switch off (perseverance) then the brain–body conversation becomes continuous. People with severe autism will focus almost entirely on this to the exclusion of what is going on outside since inside is safe, always the same. Occasionally they may fixate on some object or activity hijacked from the world outside (like tearing bits of paper or closing doors) but this will not be a true interest in their surroundings; rather they use the stimulus they receive from this to 'feed' the perseverant brain. (See Figure 5.1.)

Before we think it is just something that affects people with ASD we need to realize that we are all involved in repetitive behaviour. Whether we are NT or autistic, the brain and body are involved in numerous and continuous conversations. For example, when we breathe in, our brain sends a message to the various muscles in our body which pattern inhalation, telling us to breathe in. If we try this deliberately we find that we cannot go on breathing in for ever. When we have expanded our lungs and drawn breath, our bodies send a sensation known as feedback back to the brain saying that our lungs are full up. This brain–body conversation is going on all the time – in the case of breathing, if it were not, we should be dead. And yet we are unaware of it unless we are involved in certain types of meditation which focus on breathing rhythm or if we have been running, in which case we 'hear' our panting.

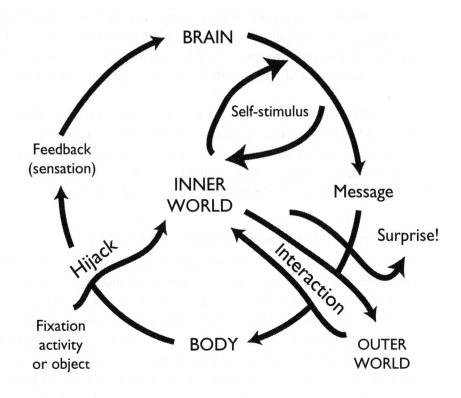

Figure 5.1 Repetitive brain–body conversation

Where we are focused – feedback

The vital question is *where* our attention is directed. Are we listening to our own internal body rhythms, to the feedback we get from deploying some object or part of our bodies? Or, in the case of fixations, have we hijacked some object or behaviour from the outside world to feed our inner world? Or is our attention focused on the world outside ourselves – on 'other'?

When a child or adult with ASD is lost in a repetitive behaviour, they are cut off from us. We say they are interested in cars or tearing paper, drawing trains, jigsaws or a construction toy.

So let us look very carefully at what Temple Grandin is saying about her childhood preoccupation with spinning coins. 'I was intensely preoccupied with the *sound* of a spinning coin. I did this because it cut out all the other sounds. Even quite loud sounds did not disturb me' (NBC Film).

It appears that what interests her is not the object itself (which is a means to an end) but the sensory feedback which she derives from its employment, what we might call the 'buzz' she gets from the activity, in this case sound. She uses this to control her environment by excluding other sounds which are, at least potentially, overwhelming.

If we say that people 'love' jigsaws and how clever they are because they can do them upside down, we may be misunderstanding the fascination of them. If we observe such people closely when they are not 'doing their thing', we may notice they are rubbing their fingertips together. In fact, such people may not be at all interested in the picture, switching off their attention as soon as the last piece goes in, as anyone will know who has tried to draw their attention to particular subjects in the picture. Watching them carefully as they do the jigsaw, it becomes clear that the fascination lies not just in the picture but in the tactile stimulus they are giving themselves in their fingertips as they pick up the individual pieces. In the middle of sensory chaos, when they are immersed in this feedback, they know what they are doing. It is noticeable that when they are upset, the way in which they set about doing the puzzle becomes more frenzied as they desperately try to avoid spinning off into fragmentation.

Other individuals will use visual feedback to establish control by 'framing' their environment or building deliberate symmetry.

A child is said to love toy cars. What he actually does when he plays with them is to put them very close to his eye and look through the windows, turning his head round slowly to view a miniature landscape. In a slippery world his view is now framed and small enough for him to be able to interpret. A child plays with plastic pipes, placing them in symmetrical patterns. When the pattern is complete he sits back and watches them with ferocious concentration. It is not the pipes he is interested in as such but the pattern, something that is familiar to his brain in an unpredictable environment.

The favourite toy of another child, who is fascinated by symmetry, is a set of plastic hexagons which can be linked into a circle. Again, it is not so much the hexagons themselves which are the object of his attention but the completed circle. Unfortunately for him, he also feels the desperate need to assemble this on the threshold of a room, where he is contained in the safety of the doorframe. This is not a good choice. His 'circle' is frequently wrecked by other people walking in and out of the room. He spends much of his life in a fury at the destruction of what is for him a part of his life-support system. (The visual feedback from a completed circle lets him know what he is doing. It is significant as a landmark that his brain recognizes.)

A suggestion that might be helpful in this case is to set up for him an area which is similarly containing (as was the doorframe), say an empty sandbox. Here he could feel safe enough to build his circles without fearing their imminent destruction. He could go away and return when he feels in need of coherence and find the intact signals he so desperately needs to reassure himself. In practice, knowing that the signals are safe usually reduces dependency on them.

Some people might want to interpret his choice of site as a deliberate desire for the destruction of those things he values, the argument being that 'as I am not worth anything, so nothing I build has value'. I have come across this apparent need to assist self-destruction once when a man who was clearly enjoying an activity would suddenly wreck it (and attack those who were near him) but I favour the interpretation that when he experienced feedback of what we would interpret as warmth and appreciation, what he actually felt was pain instead of pleasure. In fact he was suffering Emotional Overload.

Each person with ASD develops their own ways of coping with the sensory disorder which is their experience of a world they share with NT people. In pursuing these repetitive behaviours and fixations, their attention is totally locked down into activities with which the brain feels safe. In so doing, they exclude the world outside. They listen in to their own body rhythms or may fixate on a sensation which they derive from the external world by 'hijacking' an object or activity from outside and using it to feed their inner world.

At its simplest, a person who is totally withdrawn and does not join in any activity they have been offered may respond by turning towards us and smiling when we respond to their breathing or sounds, or sigh to their rhythm. This is something their brain recognizes not only as benign but also interesting. It is as if, being hard-wired in, it is a stimulus that is familiar and does not threaten them with overload but is also intriguing since it is 'their sound' but they did not make it. Often, they will hold out their hands and smile. They are longing to communicate but cannot do so until we can learn the language they use to talk to themselves. Somehow through our interaction we have to find a way of showing a person that we understand the 'rules' by which they survive. We have to show that we value them.

At its simplest, heavy breathing may be just one of a number of ways a person talks to themselves. A young man taps his fingers. When I echo back the rhythm of his tapping we develop an elaborate finger-hopping game, which catches his attention in a way he clearly enjoys.

A man bangs his head on the floor. When I bang on the wall, he recognizes 'his rhythm' and stops banging to see what I am doing. As I have his attention, I bang again and we start a conversation out of what had previously been self-harm. This almost always works. It can be seen in the video *Learning the Language* (Caldwell 2002b). Gabriel gets annoyed at a time when I am using a vibration unit with him and he wants to stand it up and balance it. He bangs the floor and I do the same. He looks up immediately. He then bangs his chest and I bang myself. He looks at me in a slightly puzzled manner and stops. His care staff tell me that normally he would have started to self-harm by banging his head on the cupboard door and bellowing.

A child comes to a sensory centre. Normally she either wanders around looking at the lights or lies on a water bed next to the entrance, with a pillow over her head. She does not engage with support staff. When I come she is on the mattress with her head at the far end under the cushion. I stand outside the door and watch. She kicks the mattress and I tap the same rhythm on the wall. She then sweeps her feet across the mattress which makes a different sound. I make a similar sound by rubbing the wall. She alternates one sound with another which builds into a fast interactive 'game'. Gradually she lifts her pillow and her head comes round to see what I am doing. We can see that she is smiling. I sit down at her level and continue to answer her rhythms and sounds on the mattress, in a way she recognizes as part of her language. She bangs a foot down; I put my left hand on it; she places her other foot on top of my hand. I complete the pile by placing my right hand on top. Clearly she is telling me she wants to play the child's game 'Building Castles'. Next, she sits up and turns round so her head is close to mine. She bangs her hands and introduces the same game, only this time played with hands instead of her feet. She is laughing. Finally she puts her arms round me and hugs me.

Another man with a very difficult behavioural history sits in his sitting room in a position where he can see the comings and goings of people through the door. In his chaotic sensory world he is desperate to know what is happening. Although his support team have worked very hard to help him and his disturbed behaviour is reduced, every now and then his anxiety explodes and he screams and bangs the walls. I sit and watch him, trying to work out how he talks to himself. What is the sensory conversation going on between his brain and body? How is he self-stimulating in a way that excludes the world outside? Particularly, *what feedback is he giving himself?*

This man stares deeply into people's eyes. (I am told he likes eye contact.) He sighs, bites his finger, moves his thumb, makes sound and rolls string between his fingers. We need to try and unravel which of these activities he is focusing on in order to protect himself from over-stimulation and which he is using as part of the ways he talks to himself (although in practice these functions may overlap).

Surprise

The most obsessional part of this man's behaviour is his string rolling. If this is interrupted he is very distressed. When he puts his face close to another person's face and stares at their eyes it does not feel like communication – it appears to see the other person as object rather than subject. There is no you and me reciprocal quality about an activity that uses a person, rather than inviting exchange with a partner. It feels more as if he is latching on to some physical attribute of them, perhaps the dark pupils. However, when he looks at them, he knows what he is doing. To break the spell we have to introduce a related stimulus which uses what he is doing (an element of his language his brain will recognize as familiar) but in a slightly different and unexpected way. We are looking for something his brain recognizes but which at the same time contains an element of the unexpected, a sort of surprise, a 'whoops factor' which shifts attention from 'self' to 'other'. Speaking of the place of this element of surprise in the process of redirection, Inge Rodbroe says, 'it's the difference, always the difference' (Rodbroe 2004).

I ask the member of his support staff whom he is staring at to flick her eyes away and back again. Immediately he recognizes this as a related but different response. It's an 'answer' in a mode that grabs his fancy. He begins to attend to her as a person/subject rather than the object of his fixation.

We echo his deep breathing, his sighs, his thumb movements and answer his sounds, placing empathy in our responses. Now that he realizes that every time he makes an utterance he will get an answer that has meaning for him, he very quickly becomes more deeply attentive. From being quite quiet his sounds become firmer and he starts to make movements and sounds and then look up round the room, engaging one of us after another. Each time he gets a response he laughs delightedly. He has moved from solitary self-stimulation to shared activity in which we are all involved. We too share his pleasure. He has completely lost interest in his obsessional string rolling and stops biting his finger. Time passes beyond the exact time when he would normally insist on his cup of tea. Interaction is more fun. And it is more fun for us too. Instead of sitting anxiously wondering quite how we are going to deflect his next outburst, we are meeting a person in a way that has not been possible before. Now we have found a way to talk to each other and enjoy ourselves together. We have put aside our reality and entered creatively into his world. He has a lot to show us.

Observation and the individual repertoire

Observation is critical. We have to really look not only at the sum total of what a person is doing but also at what is happening in the most minute detail. We need to know everything they are doing, because each person's body speaks their particular language. When we use Intensive Interaction we look at the whole repertoire, the whole landscape of behaviour, all the feedback a person is giving themselves, everything that is special for this particular individual. What are they doing? Where are they doing it? Especially, how they are doing it will give us an insight into how they are feeling.

The landscape of their self-stimulation and communication will include both closed-circuit, inwardly directed messages, the way they talk to themselves and also open, outwardly directed messages, all of which together will form a particular terrain with which the brain is familiar –

and which therefore does not present as threatening and likely to contribute to overload.

This inner language, which consists of behaviour (in its widest sense) with which the brain is familiar, will include the following:

1. Undirected non-verbal utterances and movements which are involuntary (for example, breathing rhythms, breath-holding explosive sounds, the sounds made by sucking saliva) but are nevertheless recognizable to the brain as part of a familiar repertoire.

2. Non-verbal utterances and gestures which are used purposefully and directed to self. These are part of the brain–body conversation through which the person self-stimulates when the brain cannot make sense of the world outside and attends to the feedback it is getting from the body. This brain–body language is how they talk to themselves.

There may also be outwardly directed language, the aim of which is to communication. This communication can be through non-verbal, pre-verbal or verbal utterances and gesture. The aim here is different: it is to bridge the gap between themselves and us. They want to inform us, to tell us something. This something may be negative – for example, a nudge to indicate we are sitting too close to them. If we do not respect this they may go on to more aggressive behaviour.

Neglecting the inner-world language

Much of the time we neglect a person's inwardly directed language. Its potential for interaction (as a recognizable stimulus which does not present a threat) has been lost since *we* do not recognize it as meaningful for us. But both inner and outwardly directed elements can be used in Intensive Interaction. Our aim is to pick up *anything at all* which has meaning for our partner's brain, which is part of their brain's familiar repertoire. We are trying to shift our partner's attention from their inner world to interaction with the world outside. To do this we need to pay total attention to what they are *actually* doing in every sense. We are searching for a pattern that fits the template of what an individual brain recognizes, their particular model.

A child aged 17 has CHARGE Syndrome and is diagnosed as autistic. He has no sight and very difficult behaviour. He does make sounds but when I echo these back he is totally unresponsive to the point at which I realize that although this has not been diagnosed, he is also completely deaf, either physically or effectively. He holds a piece of sheet foam in his hands with circular holes cut into it and runs his fingers round the holes. This is how he talks to himself, giving himself tactile feedback, the pattern of which is a circle. Each time he makes a sound, I make a circular movement on his arm. He starts to laugh, especially when I reverse the direction, feeding in the circle pattern he recognizes but containing the element of surprise, anti-clockwise to his clockwise. I leave him playing with his father. He is very moved and says that it is the first time he has been able to play with his son. A couple of months later, during which he has continued the interactions, he reports that his son who had been so disturbed is now so happy.

Recognition of movement patterns, even when presented in a different place, is relatively common. I recall three individuals, all of whom it was thought were impossible to interact with. A schoolgirl rotated a plastic windmill and laughed when I made circles with my finger in the air. A man spent his time rotating the dial of a toy telephone. He thought it extremely funny when I made the same movement on his wrist. The third was a man with no sight and with extremely distressed behaviour to the point at which personal care had become hazardous for his staff. He constantly licked his lips with a circular movement. He would not let me touch his hand so I drew the movement on his foot. He started to laugh so loudly that his support staff came running from all over the house. No-one had heard him laugh before.

All three people thought it especially funny when I changed to 'drawing' their movement in the opposite direction. They became deeply attentive, since they knew that I had recognized the template that was significant for them. It felt like we shared the joke of my having cracked their code. We were *complicit* in what had meaning for them. Watching a piece of video where a woman had a similar highly amused response to my finding out how to interact with her, a colleague observed that it looked as though she was saying, 'At last, after forty years, someone has stumbled on to how to talk to me.'

Humour is a bridge between partners which both may use to cross the divide. The doorway begins to open, the relationship to crystallize into an equal partnership as our partner offers new and often surprisingly humourous material to test us out. Robert says of Walker that he will quite deliberately tease his father, mistyping 'i' for 'l' and laugh at him. This is not a mistake, the body language of deliberation and referring back (how far can I push him?) defines the ploy as a 'wind-up' for fun. Once a woman who was hitting herself realized that every time she did so, I tapped my nose, she started to introduce all sorts of different arm movements. Every time I got them right, she laughed.

A man with ASD and extreme behavioural difficulties responds to his sounds being used to talk to him. In the video *Learning the Language* (Caldwell 2002b) a member of his support team describes how he begins to push the boundaries, making higher and different sounds until they begin to laugh together as she protests, 'I can't do that one!' He has capped her joke. A similar situation arose when I was working with another man who scribbled. Every time he scribbled, I scribbled. He began to smile and drew up his chair to be nearer. Next time he scribbled deliberately not on his paper but on the table and grinned at me. My reaction was the same, laughter and 'I can't do that one!' (Ignore whether the table mattered – in the scale of things it didn't. Overriding this, he who is deeply disturbed was able to share a joke with a stranger.) In the game of brinkmanship he was the clear winner.

For all of us, anything quirky or odd attracts our attention – the brain needs to look it over and assess the 'risk factor'. We might describe this sense of humour as relief in being 'able to share' but it seems to be more than that when our partner adds to the joke, extending it by referring back to us with something new and looking at us to see what we make of this. This is precisely what we do when we want to make friends: we test them out to see if they are the same as us. There is an enormous feeling of relief when our partners 'get this' and delight that here is someone with whom we can share what is in effect our childhood playground which lives on in all of us. They will not laugh at us but with us. Our boundaries expand as we learn to trust each other.

We find ourselves in a playground, a space that allows us freedom to explore our partner's feelings by looking at *how* they respond. We need to look and listen, not just with our eyes and ears but with all our senses so that every part of us is aware not just of physical movement but also changes in tension and behaviour. Where do they withdraw and what helps develop their confidence? For example, a man who drew road plans was afraid when we added cars, until we drew a car park to contain them. From this we learn that he could not cope with the unpredictability of movement he did not control. It caused him stress which started the turmoil which so upsets him. But the man who scribbles described above is able to initiate an enquiry, he is probing my feelings. Provided we stay within the parameters of a person's own language and themes we can begin to open out the space between us, learning the shape of each other's strengths and sensitivities. We can build a shared world in which we feel safe and can have fun.

Christopher

So let us return to Christopher. I meet him with his mother, father and support partner at the day centre. His father sits beside him and I ask him to screw up his fist like Christopher's and place it where Christopher can see it. They start to talk using hand movements, opening and closing their hands and pointing fingers. Christopher is clearly pleased when he makes a movement and gets a reply. He begins to smile. When we all put out our fists in the middle of the circle in which we are sitting, he looks round at us smiling, one after the other. He nudges me with his foot. This opens out into a stamping game which he finds hilarious. He begins to make sounds. I return these and, when he looks up at my face, I cover it with my hand and suddenly remove it and put it back again, looking and hiding before eye contact becomes an issue. We have found a way of making contact and particularly of having fun together in a way we all understand and enjoy. It is not only Christopher who is released from constraint. We have found pleasure in each other's company.

Intensive Interaction and attention to the hypersensitivities

Intensive Interaction is clearly a successful way of communicating with Christopher but there is also another issue which relates to his ASD. Is he hiding his eyes so closely behind his hand because he enjoys watching his fingers move, keeping the sensory invasion of the world outside at bay by using the movement to give himself stimulatory feedback, or hiding his face related to a hypersensitivity to light? When I suggest to his parents that they try a green lightbulb in his room at home, it appears that under these altered conditions he can sit up and look at the world around him. He does not need to hold his hands in front of his face. So we now have a way of both reducing the sensory stimulus to which he is hypersensitive *and* improving his ability to enjoy interaction and communicate. Christopher has now been tested for and is encouraged to wear Irlen lenses. His interest in his surroundings is improving – for example, he will more often make sounds and point to things that catch his fancy.

Video

The use of video is very helpful in improving practice since at the time of an interactive session one may be so absorbed in what one is doing that it is extremely easy to overlook the significance of some of one's own responses and one's partner's behaviours. The rather longer meeting I had with Pranve was videotaped by the speech therapist, offering an opportunity to analyse in detail what was going on.

Authorities have mixed views about the use of video recording, some feeling that this is an invasion of privacy. Very occasionally a person will find it invasive – and their need must be respected. One woman not only ushered the member of staff wielding the video camera out of the door but also seized my notebook and threw it out of the window. She made her requirement for privacy abundantly clear. Any intervention which she felt treated her like an object was off-limits. However, this is extremely rare. I can only recall one other person who objected, a young man whom I wanted to photograph in order to supply photos for a communication system. His whole face screwed up. I asked him if cameras were 'bad'. Although no-one had heard him speak, he said 'yes' quite clearly.

Everything we do needs to be related to the needs of a particular individual and these should be respected. In the rare cases where a person has shown a negative response to being filmed, this has been immediately discontinued. On the other hand there is urgent need for self-scrutiny so that we can constantly be improving our practice, since what gives more positive enrichment to the lives of people with ASD than anything else is when they can have free and enjoyable communication (through a language they understand) with the people who are part of their lives. Support workers can become real friends on equal partnership terms. Learning a person's language truly values what is important to a particular person and both partners can learn to enjoy each other this way. Video helps us to pick up where we have missed out on potential elements for communication.

Pranve

We may need to make a distinction between repetitive behaviour that is a part of the way a person talks to themselves, and behaviour that is a direct response to anxiety. Anxiety behaviour is a coping strategy. For example, a person who keeps taking themselves off to the toilet may be getting out of a situation that is overloading them and giving themselves space to process or, if they are in a new place, they may simply be reassuring themselves in a small closed space with low arousal: 'Under these new circumstances if I am scared, I relieve myself, because then I know what I am doing'. Both options are part of a person's body language and need to be taken into account.

Living at the end of an airport runway, Pranve is a very anxious young man, hypersensitive to sound and with a number of distressed behaviours. Having introduced myself to him by making his sounds outside his front door *before he can see me*, he leads me into the sitting room and we sit down together, myself on the sofa and he on a comfy chair at right angles to me. Although he sits beside me his body language betrays his anxiety and he is slightly turned away from me. He is anxious about the planes passing over; every time he hears them he turns towards the left, lifting his head to the sound. The noise hurts his ears.

Apart from his soft triple sound, 'er-er-er', which is just audible, Pranve talks to himself by rubbing his fingers on both hands. (His brain says to his body 'rub', and the feedback is the friction this produces. When he is doing this he knows what he is doing.) I start to work with his sounds and also with his hand movements on his right hand and then combine the two, tracing the 'shape' of his sound on his arm. He turns his body towards me and grins and offers me the ball of string he keeps under his arm – and then takes it back again quickly and stuffs it into his T-shirt. His sounds increase in volume but he is still concerned about the noise of a plane coming in to land (they come about every four minutes) which makes a break in our interactions. When I try to restart too quickly, he makes a brief effort to thump my arm, simply letting me know that he cannot cope if I do not respect his need for space to process when he is anxious. I bang the arm of the sofa, letting him know I have got his message and he settles again. Our interactions resume. As he becomes more and more involved with our interactions, he ceases to be worried by the noise of the planes and no longer looks up as they pass overhead.

To refer back to Figure 5.1 (p.102), Pranve's brain sends a message to his body saying rub your fingers and his body gives feedback to the brain in the form of tactile sensation. His brain repeats the message ('perseverates') and so the brain–body conversation continues. He also listens to his own 'er-er-er' sounds but these are, as we shall see, potentially communication sounds and develop into proto-speech and eventually into recognizable words, carried on song. What shifts his attention from the inside to the outside world is the surprise of hearing his sounds and seeing his movements made by a source which is 'not self'. His attention is directed outwards to locate where they are happening.

Looking at the video later on, I see that I have only picked up part of another sequence. When Pranve is especially anxious he turns to the standard light in the corner between us and touches both the fringe and then the stand itself. When he does this he knows what he is doing. This is repeated several times but I still do not understand the significance for him of the double movement and I only touch the fringe. To complete the cycle he takes my hand and physically touches the stand. (As part of the primal human behaviour whereby we all need the parent to confirm our behaviour, already referred to in the section on Intensive Interaction (p.100), Pranve wants me to confirm the pattern of this anxiety behaviour so he can move on. I do emphasize that this is not treating Pranve as an infant but simply that we are both taking part in what is an embedded cycle of human behaviour.) When I still do not understand, he moves off to his room and we have a break.

About ten minutes later, Pranve is kneeling on the floor of the hall, banging the wall. I bang back. His father observes that when he does this they try to stop him, that he sees that they have been 'against' him but what I am doing is 'for' him. I reply to the effect that what is uppermost in my mind is the turmoil that is going on in Pranve's brain and how he is trying to control this by giving his mind a focus in banging the wall. What I am trying to do, by echoing his sound, is to shift his attention from his inner distress to the world outside himself, so that his brain is put in the position of saying, 'Hey, that's my sound (or rhythm) but I did not make it.' I want him to look outside himself for the source of 'his' utterances.

Pranve bangs his feet and I bang mine. He smiles and his father comments that he is 'Happy now'.

Pranve takes out his ball of string and throws it back into the sitting room so that, knowing where it is, he will be safe if he comes in and collects it. He then stands up, comes in, picks up his string and stamps his feet. I stamp back. He laughs and goes and puts his arms round his mother, puts his head on her shoulder and hugs her. She rubs his back.

In the next sequence, Pranve's triple 'er-er-er' resolves into rhythmic precursors of the words 'Where's-Char-lene?' (Charlene is his sister.) He starts to clap his hands. I clap back. He responds, then looks away. I wait until he looks up before answering. We laugh together. Together we have got beyond the stage of wondering what to do next. Our common language is a passport into each other's worlds. It gives access to how we feel and sharing feelings is a quick way to make friends and allies.

After lunch we are in the kitchen. Pranve positions himself very carefully so as to be in the optimum position relative to me in his next burst of activity. He brings a bouncy high chair over and sits in front of me with his back towards me, bouncing up and down, clearly showing me that he wants to be bounced. I wait until he makes a sound and then bounce the rhythm. He catches on to the idea that if he makes a sound I will bounce him very quickly. He smiles and then twists round towards me and we share the joke. He is starting to sing although at first it is not clear what. He struggles with a phrase and after several attempts it comes, the first line of 'Baa, Baa, Black Sheep'. His lip wobbles as he tries to get the next line. Clearly he knows what he wants to do but is having trouble organizing the rhythm and music. On video this is very obvious. A few notes come first and then a tentative first line of the song with the words. He keeps at it and finally he sings the first two lines very clearly. Whether or not this is 'age-appropriate', for him it is a magnificent achievement and he is clearly delighted. His face shines with pleasure. The speech therapist who is filming says she has never heard him use words so distinctly before.

Before I leave, Pranve retires to the front room. This is his retreat, so I do not go in to say 'Goodbye' but, when outside, spread my fingers on the window pane near where he is sitting. He looks at his fist, then opens his hand slowly and matches my fingers through the glass. In five hours we have been on a long journey together.

Christopher, Pranve and finally Gabriel.

Gabriel

Gabriel and I meet as a result of the decision to make a training film (*Learning the Language* – Caldwell 2002b) which will follow the course of an intervention using Intensive Interaction over three days, starting from the situation of never having met the person who is to be my partner. He is chosen by other people as being one of the most difficult individuals they know to work with. Although Gabriel's mother has written a fascinating book about his growing up (Rankin 2000), when we meet I know nothing about this, or him, except his name, that he has ASD, epilepsy and the reputation of being totally cut off. The psychologists said, 'If you can work with Gabriel you can work with anybody.'

After making the film, I found a review of his mother's book (Rankin 2000): 'He is incontinent, has no speech, shows no spontaneous affection, bangs his head and demands constant attention.'

A senior nurse tutor of one of the nurse training hospitals subsequently told me she had tried to work with him for two years and failed to get a single positive response.

Gabriel is unable to sit down with anyone or focus on any activity. He does not make eye contact. He bangs his head on the wall and bellows with distress. Most of his time is spent rubbing his fingers or flicking an object such as rubber gloves, string or grass with his right hand, usually on to the side of his left hand. This is the way he talks to himself, it is where his attention is and when he is doing this he knows what he is doing. It is interesting that the finger rubbing and the objects are interchangeable. It is not the object itself that is important. It is a tool to provide him with the stimulus he needs.

Working from the present

I deliberately do not take a long history as I need to work from what is happening now. As a consequence of this, when I start work with Gabriel as my partner and before I have spotted how it is that he (or any other person who is going to be my communication partner) is talking to himself, I feel at a loss. What am I doing here, thinking I am going to be able to make a connection with someone who seems to be, at best, oblivious to my presence or taking evasive action or even hostile? But I have learned that I need to go through this stage of bewilderment in order to empty myself of my own agenda, what I expect, so that I can focus more deeply on what it is that has meaning for my partner. This is the process of learning their language, a process of trial and error, recognizing where I get it wrong, learning from this and moving on gradually. One can think of it as like climbing a cliff, trying out first one route and then another. What I want to know is which of my interventions speaks to my partner – which one he or she recognizes and enjoys. Which one grabs their attention?

Using the personal code

Suppose that I have ASD and severe learning disabilities. I cannot make sense of the kaleidoscope world I live in. My environment swirls round me and noises boom in my ears. Maybe my skin hurts and I cannot make out what is going on. Sometimes I am swept by painful surges from my own nervous system. When these are more than I can bear I try banging my head or lashing out at the people/things that overload my senses, to stop the over-stimulation. I retreat to my own world and focus on a particular sensory stimulus. If I concentrate hard enough I can lock out the disturbing sounds and movements and demands which so torment me. My brain attends to my hard-wired familiar patterns and themes, those which it recognizes and does not find threatening because they are a part of my landscape. If you want to talk to me you are going to have to use what amounts to my personal code to get through to me.

Moving attention from 'self' to 'other'

The journey from self to other is illustrated in Figure 5.2. The self-absorbed self moves from recognition to attention and from attention to engagement, becoming increasingly aware of the world outside themselves and interactive with it.

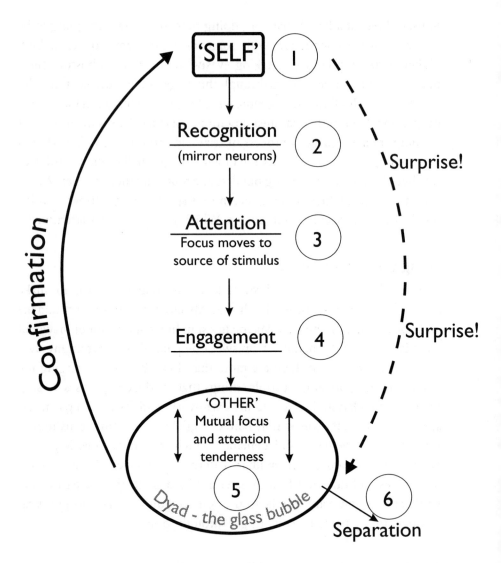

1.   The self is listening to its own stimuli.

2.   The self recognizes the replica stimuli made by 'other' through its mirror neurons.

3.   The self attends to the sounds or movements made by other. The self realizes that every time it makes a movement or sound, other will respond.

4.   Self and other are engaged in partnership – they refer back to, and confirm, each other.

5.   Shared pleasure moves into affective exchange and an intimate conversation in the dyad. The movement from 'self' to 'other' is driven by surprise; the surprise of recognizing 'my sound/movement', 'part of my repertoire' in the world outside itself. Focus shifts from self to other. Other confirms self's initiatives.

6.   Other's self-esteem is raised by being valued. Self and other separate.

Figure 5.2 Moving attention from 'self' to 'other'

Recognition

First of all I have to recognize that what you offer me is related to the familiar patterns of my repertoire. It doesn't have to be exactly the same but it must contain elements which are sufficiently close to my template to 'ring a bell' for me, to make me pause in my self-stimulation (for example, the rhythms of my sounds used as patterns on my skin). Meltzoff says of infants (and the same is true for adults):

> Although infants cannot see their faces, their faces are not unperceived by them. They can monitor their lips and tongue movements through proprioception and compare this felt identity to what they see. Metaphorically we can say that perception and proprioception speak the same language, there is no need for associating the two through prolonged learning because they are intimately bound at birth. (Meltzoff 1999)

Recent work has shown that we have in our brains a network of nerve cells that are known as 'mirror neurons' towards the back of the head (Rizzolatti and Arbib 1998; Rizzolatti et al. 1995). This network fires not only when we perform an action ourselves but also when we see someone else perform the same activity (Astafiev et al. 2004). If you copy me I know that it is me you are copying. Furthermore some of these mirror neurons are crossmodal so I also recognize the 'pattern' when it is presented through a different sense (Kohler et al. 2002).

The work on mirror neurons is ongoing and, to some extent, conflicting. For example, an indirect study of the activity of mirror neurons (as measured by the suppression of a brain wave known as the mu wave when the mirror neurons are active) suggests that a control group of neurotypical people had suppressed mu waves when they moved, and when observing movement on video. A matched group of people with Asperger's Syndrome had suppressed mu wave activity when they moved – but not when they saw others move. These observations are difficult to reconcile with the imitative interactions observed and eager responses on the part of hundreds of people on the spectrum, to seeing part of their *own* repertoire reflected back to them. It would appear that there is selective recognition of personal activities or parts of those activities even, for example, when their rhythm is presented in a different mode. But there is less or no recognition when the activity they witness is not, so to speak, part of their 'hard-wired in' repertoire. In his paper on imitation, mirror neurons and autism, Williams points out that while those on the spectrum do not on the whole engage in repetition, 'this is not so of the well known repetitive and stereotyped behaviours. These may be copied from others, including words and phrases (echolalia) and sometimes actions.' He goes on to say that 'these are mimicked without regard to their normal goals and meaning' (Williams *et al.* 2001).

I think it would be more true to say that while they may not have a meaning in 'our world' reality, imitations function as part of an attempt to communicate on the part of people with ASD. For example, imitation (as opposed to initiation) most often occurs in conjunction with referring back – that is, when the person has recognized some element which has significance for them and is trying it out as a way of communicating. It should not be seen in abstract – as it so often is under laboratory conditions where the testee is offered a video of an unrelated activity – but as part of the process of trying to communicate. Furthermore, echolalia can be an attempt to use what speech is available to express a need as was seen in the section on restricted speech. Nadel explores the imitative capacities of young children with autism and suggests that

> the lack of attraction for novel experiences may extensively limit the building of strong and automatic motor representations but does not limit low-level imitations. Using the mental age of the children instead of their chronological age she demonstrated that the developmental path of children with ASD is similar to that of children not on the spectrum, consistent with the idea that children with autism are not specifically impaired in imitation.

She goes on to say that

> there was a significant relationship between the level of imitation and imitation recognition. Those children who were good imitators all recognized being imitated...reinforcing the hypothesis that the communicative function of imitation emerges very early from the intermeshing of imitating and being imitated. (Nadel *et al.* 2004)

To try and put this simply I shall invent two fictitious characters called Jim and Tom. If we see Jim imitate Tom, we know that he has recognized what Tom is doing. So let us suppose that Jim flaps his hands repetitively; this is the way he talks to himself. If he sees Tom flap his hands he imitates him, because this is something his brain recognizes and which he can pull out of the sensory chaos he lives in. But Jim does not imitate Tom if Tom performs an alternative action or, as is frequently used in tests, shows him another action such as putting a brick in a box on video, because it is outside the well-worn path of his repertoire. It has no significance for him. It is only when Jim recognizes what it is that he uses to talk to himself, that he can use this to interact with Tom.

We know that Jim is not just flapping his hands randomly if his reply is contingent – if he times his responses in relation to Tom's flap and especially if he imitates and refers back to Tom, looking to see what he makes of it.

To generalize, much of what we see as low-level repetitive behaviour is part of the communication system which at present is being used to communicate with self rather than other. Only when 'other' (us NTs) uses it to interact can the person restore their behaviour to its rightful function as part of the interactive system.

It should be pointed out that the type of activity which constitutes complex repetitive behaviour is more commonly found (but not exclusively) at the least able end of the spectrum. Furthermore, response has to relate to what the person is doing *now*. The problem with using videotapes and audio tapes of a person's behaviour to play back to them is that the stimuli are not contingent to the present (Oberman *et al.* 2005).

Returning to Christopher, Pranve and Gabriel, all are deeply withdrawn into their own worlds, on the run from the torrent of our-world stimuli to which they are hypersensitive. Yet, in spite of their extremely withdrawn state, Christopher recognizes when his father sits beside him and uses his hand movements and Pranve recognizes the familiar pattern of his sounds when I used them to introduce myself *before we met*. On video it is clear that, when Gabriel first becomes aware of my sitting near and flicking gloves in time to his rhythm, he does not look at me but sneaks the occasional glance to see what I am doing. (It is only later – when realizing that the rhythm of 'flick and touch' is so important to him that I use vibration to provide him with the stimulus in which he is interested but in a different way – that he is surprised and looks at me for the first time.)

And yet when I have learning disabilities and ASD, even when I am deeply fixated on my self-stimulation, talking to myself through my brain–body language, there is part of my brain which remains on alert, a periscope from my inner world sweeping the horizon for events or activities which it recognizes, an early warning system for me to take notice and pay attention. In the middle of trying to make sense of the sensory chaos *here is something I can latch on to without the strain of having to try and interpret it*. (Donna Williams tells us in an NBC film that when she hears one of her own sounds it is like being thrown a life-belt in a stormy sea. What she is describing is a life-threatening situation, being rescued from the danger of drowning. The struggle to keep up with her sensory situation is that important.)

Gaining attention

At this stage if you are engaged in an activity I recognize, it is only the activity I am interested in and not you. You remain an object. Bruce Durie points out that, lower down the evolutionary scale, if we met an object all we needed to know was whether we should eat it, run from it or mate with it. As we climbed up the evolutionary ladder we also learned to make use of objects; we turned them into tools (Durie 2005). At the beginning of our interaction, Gabriel is using the rubber gloves as a tool to give himself a stimulus which is significant and non-threatening.

Looking at this from the point of view of the partner with autism, what I am interested in is the stimulus which you are providing me and not necessarily you yourself. However, although what you are doing is not personal, it does start to build a bridge which will enable me to cross over to the world outside. My attention begins to shift. At least there is something out there which it is possible for me to investigate, a marker or talisman which I can rely on, since it will not threaten to break up and cause overload and fragmentation. Maybe there is something in the scary outside world I can focus on and therefore know what I am doing.

In the dynamic that we are setting up, it is not just I who will learn to pay attention to you, but you will have to give me your whole attention in order to see what is happening.

So what do we mean by attention? This is a question that appears to have a simple answer; I turn to you or listen to you, etc. But to give someone total and intimate attention is on another scale. When the famous photographer Cartier-Bresson was asked how it was that his photographs managed to capture such depth of feeling, he replied that for him, it was having 'eyes and hands and heart in the same frame'.

To give total attention means concentrating everything one has in one's partner, unencumbered by one's own expectations and needs. My focus is not just external, looking at what you are doing, your movements and listening to your utterances. It is more than that. In one sense it is about priorities.

A support worker said to me, 'I used to come to work thinking about what I had to do that day, sort the laundry, cut John's toenails, etc., but now I come in and think, "How can I make this a nice day for John?"'

Perhaps even more pertinently, another said, 'I see it's not about "doing to", but "being with".'

So what is the difference and why is presence so important?

Obviously what we are talking about is more than physical presence since we can be physically present and at the same time absent, if our mind is on other things. So our mind has to be present; we need what is known as 'mindfulness'. We also have to be attuned, the sort of attitude that Pranve's father was talking about when he said that instead of being 'against' Pranve when he was upset, trying to control him, we needed to be 'for him', empathizing with his situation and, especially, how he feels. This is not quite the same as imagining how he feels. In particular it requires that we empty our selves, putting away our own agendas and become receptive to other.

I don't want to make this sound too difficult. Some people are just naturally good at it; they slide into such an attitude of acceptance easily. Others have to work at being present, making a conscious decision to welcome our partners into our inner world of affect. There is a delicate balancing act. At the same time as I empty myself I also have to open up to being a living responding person for Pranve. At its best we enter what can only be described as a creative mutuality, where we resonate with each other. Here we are always aware of each other and responsive as we extemporize to each other's initiatives. Curiously we find that as we empty ourselves, we find our self more deeply. In a personal sense, the practice of meditation has increased my capacity to attend and be present. Others will find different ways. We can at least start by being aware of the necessity of what a speech therapist called 'intimate attention'.

To return to the person with ASD: my brain is cluttered with unprocessed images and sounds and feelings and information and I have learned to be afraid of fragmentation with its unpleasant and painful effects. I only pay attention to the limited vocabulary of objects and effects I recognize from my own world in the world outside. These have meaning for me. When I begin to recognize that I will always get a meaningful response from you to my initiatives, I start to look out for them. I develop an expectation that when I make an utterance or movement, you will answer me. Now when I see or hear or feel you start to engage with me using the language I recognize, I will respond. We will alternate, as in conversation.

There will be an alteration in my body posture and facial language. This can be very subtle, especially if the person has severe or profound learning disabilities, felt rather than seen, a change in tension and timing as the partners' initiations are brought into sync with each other, an invitation followed by a pause for a response. When it comes, recognition is signalled by a slight relaxation – as if the partner's body is saying, 'Ah, that's what I have been waiting for.' I will shift round to place myself in the optimum position to receive your replies to me just as Christopher, Pranve and Gabriel all turned towards their partner and started to smile. Their body posture and faces became more relaxed.

Engagement

And then comes the shared feeling and excitement of sharing, making an initiative, a sound, movement or action and looking back to see what our partner makes of it. 'Yes! Now! You and me together, I'll show you, you show me – and we can share the things we care about!'

At this stage, engagement can move into bonding in the dyadic state but before we discuss this we need to look at how we can keep this level of interaction going and what happens if it goes stale.

What is it that shifts attention to engagement, from the standpoint where I just notice *what* you are doing to the situation where I become attentive to you and desire to engage with you *as person*, to offer you my interests to see what you think about them, to refer back to you?

By now my brain has an expectation that you will answer me using my language, the vocabulary that I understand, in a way that has meaning for me. But suppose you start to reply with a sound I recognize and then alter the rhythm slightly? My brain is surprised and it is this surprise which hardens my attention (which you already have) to try to make out what is happening. The surprise, *which is a discontinuity in expectation*, will move from 'that's my sound but I did not make it' to 'that's my sound but it sounds a bit different' or 'is presented in a different mode' or even 'in a different context'. One way or another, something I expected to happen happens differently or even, perhaps, does not happen. The brain becomes even more alert.

The discontinuity in expectation

At this stage surprise can be visible on the face. Pupils enlarge, the eyes widen and darken or occasionally the jaw may drop: 'Wow!'

A woman has extreme self-injury and sometimes attacks those around her. Occasionally she has days when she sniffs people's hair. Otherwise she runs away from contact. She self-injures, banging her face hard and repeatedly to the point at which the cheekbone is exposed. I stand well away from her. It takes about 20 minutes before she realizes that every time she hits herself, I tap my face. She is astonished and her jaw drops until she is open-mouthed. ('That is my movement but I didn't do it.')

She hits herself more gently and then looks at me to see what I will do. I tap my cheek; she responds. Gradually I am able to walk over to her, leading her into an exchange where if she taps one side of her face, I tap the other. She is laughing. Over time she becomes extremely responsive to this type of interaction. Her wound heals. All that is left of this behaviour now is that she sometimes rubs the scar. A video shows this woman, who was previously unable to make contact with anyone outside herself, collapsing with laughter into her partner's arms after an interactive session.

In biological terms, surprise and even humour are at the very mild end of the spectrum of fear. From the standpoint of survival it is absolutely critical that our brains pick up any event which potentially offers a threat, even if it is just something odd or quirky, a faint niggle that it cannot immediately interpret and carries with it the potential of threat (Carter 1998). At the same time we build up alliances with those who will support us. Humour under these circumstances is the relief that here is someone I can play with who will not laugh at me – that is, exclude me from the group. I shall introduce something new to explore the possibility of bonding further with them. Humour comes as a reaction, relief, we share our laughter. Even if I find something funny on my own, my first thought is who I can share it with. They will be my ally in what amounts in biological terms to a hostile environment. Whether we are autistic or NT we need to be able to share those things we find fun or funny with our friends. Deliberately playing a game which both parties enjoy, especially if it involves building up anticipation and sharing the unexpected distortions, is a way of extending this. Shared humour is the cement of friendship.

Another woman smacks her feet down on the pavement. Walking behind, I copy the sound as I bang my feet down. I can see she is listening by a very slight adjustment of the tension in her shoulders viewed from the back. After building up her expectation, with the next step I take, I place my shoe quietly on the pavement. She swings round laughing immediately, sharing the joke. Nind and Hewett (1994) describe using the 'burst-pause' technique where an intervention is followed by a pause which develops expectation (Meltzoff and Moore 1992).

One might object that some people with ASD seem to have absolutely no sense of what we call danger. (I think the difference in these cases is that what *we* call 'danger' comes from the outside world which they have learned to shut off, whereas what they have been responding to is the 'surprise-and-therefore-potential risk' which is presented *within* the language of their personal repertoire.)

'Ringing a bell'

The element of surprise which we introduce may be not quite the same as part of the person's normal repertoire, just a little different but a sufficiently related part of their language to 'ring a bell'. With Pranve I 'sketch' the rhythm of his sounds on his arm. His response is gradually to draw out from himself first the rhythm of sounds and then eventually distinct and clear words. Christopher comes back with something completely different; he nudges my shoe with his. With Gabriel there is a particular point at which he stops just flicking and repeatedly shakes his string and then turns towards me and waits for a response before continuing. At this stage I know that he knows that if he initiates an activity, I will answer him. He moves from here to intimate gaze – and from gaze to turning away and banging the sink and looking back to me to see what I make of it. This is generalization. He knows I will answer if he shakes his string. How about if he bangs the sink? People with ASD are not supposed to be able to do this.

Another effect of lowering the stress level is that the brain is able to pay attention to aspects of its sensory experience which it had been unable to decipher up until this point.

> The timing of the seminar [on Intensive Interaction] could not have been better for us as it was just three days before we were embarking on our fifth attempt at toilet training our severely autistic daughter.
>
> Jenny is five, has very little language and displays very challenging behaviour. Two days in and things weren't going well at all. Indeed, the teaching assistants at school were ready to give up and try again next year. On the third day I had to wash eight complete changes of clothes and I was getting desperate.
>
> After tea I took Jenny into the downstairs loo with me. I got her to sit on the potty and I sat on the toilet. Jenny was totally disinterested and got off and started playing with the taps. This was something all too familiar and I needed to get her attention. I asked Jenny to sit again and eventually she did after a little protest. At that point Jenny started making a clicking noise with her tongue and twisting her fingers. I tried to make the same noise whilst wiggling my fingers too. Immediately Jenny looked up, almost amazed and started to laugh. The clicks continued for a while and I tried to keep up, but couldn't. In the end I started clicking my fingers. Jenny thought this was really funny and tried to click her fingers. The noise wasn't loud enough for her so she started clapping. We then went into a wonderful clapping game which got quite elaborate.
>
> At this point Jenny's attention was absolutely on me and her eye contact was fantastic. I very quietly asked Jenny to 'do a wee'. Jenny looked away and for a few seconds. I thought I had lost her. She appeared to concentrate and then stood up and looked in the potty. To both our amazement there was a small amount of urine in the potty. I cheered and Jenny beamed at me. We had been in the loo for about 45 minutes, but what a result!
>
> And that was it! From that moment on Jenny made the connection. The very next day she was dry all day and has remained so. She still insists on a nappy for poos, but we are working on that.
>
> Her support worker, Mary, attended the seminar too and was keen to try the technique on Jenny for herself. Jenny was lying on the floor in her brother's bedroom with the curtains closed. Mary went in and lay on the floor herself and tried to apply the technique. Twenty minutes later she came out of the room in tears! Jenny had given her a hug – the first time in two years. She says that Jenny is much calmer with her now and that they have a much better relationship.

Jenny's normal experience of life is one of chaotic and frightening sensory input. She simply cannot make sense of what is going on, either in the world outside or even from her own body feedback. However, as soon as she learns and sees signals that are significant, have meaning for her, her stress level falls. She begins to be able to make connections with the internal messages from her bladder to her brain.

It is not in any sense that Jenny is unwilling to be toilet trained, in fact she is proud of this achievement. It is not even that she is deliberately shutting off from her body messages, rather that she just cannot decode them while there is so much muddle going on in her sensory world. Jenny's capacity to relate to the outside world also shows a dramatic improvement. She hugs her support worker and is much calmer. Her mother says her life has changed.

When we use their language we decrease the stress level rooted in their struggle to make sense of an alien world. My experience is that they long to communicate. Using their language liberates them from the constraints imposed by environmental stress and they respond, quite often with joy.

Intensive Interaction and stress reduction

One of the greatest benefits of using Intensive Interaction is that as the stress level abates, the brain begins to work more effectively. As the stress is reduced, relaxation is accompanied by a greater capacity to understand more complex speech such as sentences with dependent clauses ('if you do that I will do this'). Depending on the level of disability, speech itself may appear – as witnessed in the long struggle Pranve had to articulate what he clearly wanted to sing, evasive little fragments on 'the tip of his tongue', his chin wobbling as he tried again and again to master the lines. What was very clear and so fascinating on video was that he knew what he wanted to do some time before it came. It took his brain time to organize delivery.

If we do not keep introducing these slight elements of surprise, an initial response may tail off. The brain drifts back into habituation, learning to ignore these signals which it has previously tested and found to be harmless.

Habituation

A man has two separate 'languages' which he uses on separate occasions. In his room, when he thinks no-one is listening, he repeatedly talks about 'going on the green bus' or 'in the red car'. When he is upset he walks in ever-decreasing circles, shouting, 'I'll get sister.'

Eventually he lashes out at someone. When the next disturbance starts, I put the two languages together: 'You'll have to get sister – in the green car.' Surprised, he stops at once. After he has thought about this for a minute he starts again. I repeat, 'You'll have to get sister in the green car.' Again he stops, but as time goes on, the combination of fetching sister in the green car becomes less effective (since it no longer surprises his brain). The next time I say, 'You'll have to fetch sister in a blue lorry.'

He stops dead again. Each time I introduce an unfamiliar element (but still in the context of his language), it refocuses his attention to the outside world in a dramatic way. What was in danger of becoming habituated was bounced back into consciousness by the unfamiliar.

As always when engaging with so-called 'challenging behaviour' we need to look for the trigger. It turns out that this man is hypersensitive to sound. Support staff are able to use this technique in order to divert his attention while another goes off to deal with the noise in the house which is upsetting him. In this situation it is not enough just to copy his language; they have to think about what he says and keep spicing up their responses with a little bit of the unexpected.

There is always a balance to be struck. If the outside world is presenting too much distraction then even if we are using their language they may retreat back into their inner world. To bring them out again we shall have to find a different way of putting together the elements of their personal language in an unexpected way – for example, sound into touch or rhythm, or in placing them in unusual and different combinations.

Long-term effectiveness of Intensive Interaction

The question is always asked: what is the outcome of this type of intervention and how effective is it in the long term? Most evidence is from individual case studies. I was asked to see a woman with very disturbed behaviour. With her perceptive care manager's permission I should like to quote a letter from her, describing her interventions of Intensive

Interaction and their outcome. (Although she uses the term 'copy', it is evident from the way she describes what she does that she goes beyond copying to response.)

> I entered her world and spoke in her language and copied her movements, proving to her that she was a person in her own right and that she was valued as such. The first time I copied her she was shocked and looked round for the source of communication. For the first time (I had been working with her for about four weeks) she gave me full eye contact and smiled at me. Each night when the others had retired we would sit there copying each other's language. I changed the rhythm, intonation, speed and began to introduce 'proper' words. To my amazement she enjoyed it all. She became much more relaxed, showed some affection and was beginning to understand and empathize with me.

> Not only did she trust me but she began transferring that trust to others. From being a lonely isolated person that refused to engage in 'our world', she is now beginning to make her own decisions. If she is hungry she will help herself to sweets or fruit. If she wants to play her keyboard she will take us by the hand and point to the keyboard. For her, giant steps!

> Where she would not allow anyone to touch her, she now voluntarily touches others in affection. She will answer questions, usually with one syllable and she doesn't hesitate to tell us to shut up if she's had enough.

On the phone her manager tells me that last Christmas this woman tore open her presents and threw them down. This year she unwrapped each one carefully and handed round some of her sweets.

An anecdote I have used before is of a young man who was supporting an extremely difficult man who was causing such problems that it was difficult to get staff to work with him. When I met his care partner two years after I had taught him how to use Intensive Interaction, he told me that when I had suggested that his partner's behaviour would improve if he 'learned to communicate with him in his language', he went away and laughed, thinking that I did not know what I was talking about. But he said he did what he was told because it was his job – and the outcome was as predicted, his partner became quiet and communicative.

The second time I talked to a parent support group, four mothers came independently and told me that using Intensive Interaction had changed their children's lives. One said, 'I now have a happy, lively child.'

Time and again, parents will say, 'she's much happier' or 'he's much quieter and calmer'.

This emotional shift continues, provided there is continuing intervention, preferably by as many people as possible of the individual's circle (and the health of the individual is maintained). Parents will express themselves grateful for being taught how to communicate with their sons and daughters with whom they now feel in touch. Challenging behaviour is reduced and may well disappear. *The long-term prospects also appear to be positive provided there is consistency.* If, however, the use of a person's language is dropped, they lose their bearings immediately. Once we have learned a person's language we must continue to use it.

At this stage staff may begin to raise practical difficulties: 'We have too much to do, we can't do this all the time.'

Normally we learn to use it quite naturally. A team leader says, 'It just becomes part of the way we interact with people', and interaction often becomes bilingual using both our languages when we communicate, as when you hear people speak Welsh with English words spattered through the sentences. Each time the person with ASD hears, sees or feels one of their initiatives, it is a marker to which they relate in our world – it makes our world safe for them.

If we stop using their language, they will lose the landmarks and regress. We have not cured the autism, only modified their environment to make it user-friendly.

(For more information on how to use Intensive Interaction see Appendix B. See also Nind and Hewett 2001.)

CHAPTER 6

The Development of Self

What do we mean by 'self'?

If we try to recall our friends or the people we know, it is not just a picture we remember. We are more than photographs. The image we have of people also contains an element of how we feel about them and how we think they feel about us. Our relationship, whatever it is, is wrapped in a mantle of 'affect'.

To try and unravel what we mean by 'self' is to plunge headfirst into well-explored but nevertheless murky philosophical waters. From the practical point of view there are three essentials. The first is the feeling *that* we are, the second is *who* we are and the third, which may not be so obvious, is *where* we are. This last is important because we may have a strong sense of self – but it may be a false self derived by taking on board the feelings of another, a state that is not attributable to deliberate imagination but rather to the fact that the reflection of our own self we receive from others is so unacceptable that we 'become' another in order to feel loved. Or we may devise a false self, in order to shield our true and more vulnerable selves.

Furthermore, our sense of ourselves may change during our life journey, so that when we read of how a person feels about themselves as a child it may differ from how this is when they have grown up – sometimes they will have a perception which is more powerful and sometimes less, depending on the vicissitudes of life and how they have reacted to them.

However, viewed from the outside, the other's self remains a constant; in essence they always taste the same. Whatever their circumstances they remain recognizable.

So I shall go for something simple. Some years ago a student who was with me said, 'Society is like an old-fashioned jar of sweets. Each person has a different flavour.'

Unfortunately the identification of self, knowing what *we* taste like, is only part of the story since we do not exist in a vacuum but in relationship. It is of all characteristics highly individual and is certainly not a matter of those with ASD having no sense of self while those of us who are NT have. In all of us, ASD and NT, this is immensely complicated by projection (displacing our sense of self, as one might speak of moving house) and introjection (taking in the sense of self of other, which one might equate with the squatters moving in) (Zeedyk 2005). However, our flavour is at least partly determined by the feedback we receive from 'other'. To speak of the 'flavour' of a person is to acknowledge the interactive part of 'self-plus-other'. Hobson says:

> Consciousness is a matter not just of thinking but of feeling. Self-con-
> sciousness (as awareness of self) involves adopting a perspective on
> oneself through identifying with the attitudes of others. (Hobson
> 2002)

One of the main thrusts of all our lives will be to establish meaningful connection and relationship between ourselves and 'other' (so that, biolog-ically speaking, we can be included in our group, essential if we are to survive in a hostile world).

We start this journey of self-identification in the familiar dialogue between mother and infant, where imitation plays a key role in the estab-lishment of intimacy, boundaries and the difference between 'me' and 'not-me'. This area has been extensively researched and I do not propose to go into it here. There is a fascinating discussion on the current state of this field in Suzanne Zeedyk's book on the transformative nature of intimacy within the dyad. She tells us that in the dyadic relationship, 'It is within the embodied process of interpersonal bargaining that boundaries are constructed and that the trust of self and other…is or is not manufac-tured' (Zeedyk 2005).

A fuller explanation of how I want us to see the term 'dyad' will be found on page 148.

The dual message

At first when we are born there is only ourselves; everything that *is* for us is an extension of self. We have no boundary and do not recognize self and other. To go back to the simple analogy of sweeties, everything tastes of me. At the moment of birth everything I react to is part of me. If this is so, instead of feeling that bright light *out there* is hurting my eyes, that sensation is a bit of me. I am protesting not at 'other-hurting-me' but 'me-hurt'. All this assumes that we do not differentiate between self and mother's heartbeat in the womb. Actually we do not know whether or not this is so. What is clear, however, is that, newly born, the long journey to find other begins at once. Amazingly, newborn babies, from 3 to 54 hours old, respond to and copy their mothers sticking out their tongues and also initiate interactions (Nagy and Molnar 2004).

As babies we make sounds and our mothers or parent figures answer us. We *feel* and *hear* ourselves saying 'Boo'. Mother answers 'Boo'. However, instead of hearing and feeling this reply, we *hear* and *see* it. Surprise. This cross-modality anchors our attention.

At the same time our brains are hard at work on setting up boundaries. When we hear our mother's confirmation our brain receives two messages. In his interesting book *Descartes' Error*, Damasio (1994) tells us:

> A special sense such as vision is processed at a special place in the body boundary, in this case the eyes. Signals from the world outside are thus double. Something you see (or hear) excites the special sense of sight as a 'non-body signal' but it also excites a 'body signal' hailing from the place in the skin where the special signal entered. When you see, you do not just see, *you feel you are seeing something with your eyes.*

When I see my mother, I not only see her but my brain receives another message saying that it is *my eyes* that are seeing her. When I hear my mother I hear the sounds she makes – but a second message tells me that it is *my ears* that are hearing mother. *So the signal I receive from her tells me both about her and also about myself.* In addition to this, I also learn from my environment. Not only does this help me to lay down boundaries (as my mother also will) but it too gives me the dual message. When I look at a plate, in addition to seeing the plate, I learn that it is my eyes that are seeing the plate.

So, in attending to what you are doing, I also learn about myself, since there is a dual message to my brain. The first tells me about what you are doing *but the second tells a different part of my brain that it is my eyes that are seeing what you are doing* (or ears that are hearing what you are doing). In paying attention to the world outside I also get feedback about myself; I learn to know that I am.

Failing to find a sense of self

Sometimes it can be very difficult to find a sense of self. This is true for all of us but is especially difficult for the person with ASD, compounded as it is by the difficulties they have in interpreting their sensory intake. This not only distorts their perception of the world outside but also, because of the second message the brain receives which tells us about ourselves, it damages the picture they have of themselves.

Gunilla Gerland (1996) describes the emptiness of her inner world – where one would expect to have some idea of what self is:

> I spent a great deal of time inside myself, as if my own world was screened off from everything else. But there was no world there inside me, *nothing more than a nothing layer*, a neither-nor, a state of being hollow without being empty or filled without being full. It just was, in there, inside myself. I was inside the emptiness and the emptiness was inside me – no more than that. It was nothing but a kind of extension of time. I was in that state and it just went on.

In *Autism and Sensing* (Williams 1998), Donna tells us she could either sense herself or the object but not herself in relation to the object.

> I could not process information from the outside and inside at the same time. I was either in a state of jolting perceptual shifts or remained in one sensory channel or the other... Either 'I' existed or 'other' existed and I did not.

I want to examine some of these difficulties which impede developing a sense of self in more detail.

The first deals with the special problems faced by people with ASD because of the difficulties they face in processing stimuli from the world outside and their internal feelings. The second follows from this and looks at the problems of knowing the boundary of self, what is 'me' and 'not me'.

The third is the problem of failure to separate from the mother, so the person, although they may be adult, is locked into the infant state. This can occur in people who are NT as well as those on the autistic spectrum but when it does it immensely complicates any therapeutic approaches. Finally, I want to look at the negative image of self which can be picked up from supporters and/or a sense of failure to 'fit in'.

Living in the kaleidoscope world

Let us continue to suppose I am autistic and my sensory intake is scrambled. It is difficult for me to receive reinforcing messages about my state of self from the world outside, that I am, if I cannot get straight messages about that which is other than me. If my interpretation of the sensory world we share – and hence my relation to it – is in chaos, I have no mirror to tell me about myself. It is going to be extremely difficult for my brain to process sensory information from the outside world in order to receive the confirmation I need for developing my sense of self.

(Sometimes the way in which people fixate on objects or part of themselves is seen as getting in the way of communication. However, ignoring it simply tells the person that you do not value what they do and stopping it leaves them vulnerable to sensory distress.)

At all costs, I may have to rely entirely on stimuli provided by my self-stimulus as being the only things my brain can recognize and so rely on. I focus all my attention on the repetitive behaviours which have meaning for me. As Temple Grandin told us earlier, if as a child she watched the spinning coin she did not have to listen to the sound that disturbed her (Arnall and Peters 1992). But because of the dual message to the brain, by cutting down on the sensory messages from outside we also cut down on information about ourselves and our boundaries, hence our information *that* we are.

The threat of invasion by sensory overload and fragmentation may become so great that the individual may project their sense of self onto some particular part of themselves – in practice, the site of their self-stimulus. Bearing in mind that we obtain our sense of knowing that we are from sensory feedback, if all that we can get from the outside world is scrambled, then our repetitious behaviours may be the only place where they can learn about ourselves, because this is where recognizable messages of sensory stimulation which tell us about ourselves come from. This is illustrated in the next two stories.

In spite of such visual clues as showing her a plate with her meal on, a woman who scratches her thumbs will not come to dinner when asked. As soon as she is asked if her 'thumbs would like to have dinner' she comes immediately and eats all her meal. I have addressed her where she feels herself to be.

Another young woman focuses all her attention on her shoulder, calling it by her name. She does nothing but look at her shoulder and say, 'I Mary', until I place my hand on her shoulder, acknowledging the place where she feels herself to be. She is then able to look at me and answer my question. A similar situation arises with a young man who is only interested in his foot. We start by massaging this and gradually spread the tactile contact back through his body so that he begins to know where he is.

A person who is fixated on an external object may project their sense of self outside the body completely. A woman only says, 'my baby doll, my baby doll'. She also, when asked if she will come to tea, can only respond if her partner asks the question, 'Will baby doll have tea?' She has displaced her sense of self, where she feels herself to be, into her companion doll. There were queries from staff as to whether going along with her fixation should be deemed to be age-inappropriate. However, ignoring it simply means that it is not possible to communicate with her since it is not addressing the place where she locates her sense of self.

Wobbly boundaries

Even my sense of my physical boundaries may be skewed. I don't know what is me or not me. In order to know who I am I need also to know who I am not. I need a boundary to mark the discontinuity between 'me' and 'not me', my 'self' and 'other'.

Donna Williams tells us that she could either 'see' or 'feel' the hand which appeared to float in front of her (Williams 1996). So, she never got the idea that it was organically part of her. For two years she wriggled it to try and get rid of the irritating object which floated in front of her.

If you don't know what is 'me' and 'not me' this has serious conse-quences since 'other' may be interpreted as threatening. A man who cannot engage with people stays in his room. He will attack anyone except one key worker who tries to enter. However, he is delighted when I respond to his body language through the glass panel in his door. The door to his room is a boundary his brain recognizes. Banging it tells him where he ends and 'other', which is not he, begins. It defines the boundary which he needs to protect himself against vulnerability to sensory and emotional overload. Another man, who normally will not come indoors but occasionally knocks on the windows and laughs if anyone looks up, comes in to engage with pleasure when we use a transparent plastic screen to help him know where he is and we are. Like the man who kicked the walls mentioned earlier, he uses touch to check up on faulty visual processing.

Failure to differentiate from mother

When this situation arises it can trigger extremely difficult behavioural problems and seriously compromises the possibility of interaction.

To understand what this means we have to take ourselves back to the newborn state. We have just emerged from the most dangerous journey that we may ever undertake in our lives. The rhythmic heartbeat that has been our background music since we were conceived has stopped. There are strange new sensations, light, heat, cold. But the most urgent and overriding need in our new world is to make contact with our source of survival, our mother, who will provide us with food and protect us during this most vulnerable period of our lives. Without her sustenance we are in danger of extinction; we shall die. All the thrust of evolutionary development is mobilized to establish this bond.

As we have already discussed, the infant does this by establishing an intense non-verbal dialogue with her. We now know that, if all goes well, almost from the moment of birth we can start to have some idea of a thing outside ourselves that responds to us, although we are not sure how conscious we are of it at the time. However, baby and mother start to play games with each other. As Suzanne Zeedyk says, if all goes well, they literally fall in love with each other. In the dyadic state, baby and mother are entranced with each other (Zeedyk 2005). Baby makes a movement or utterance and the mother responds. She confirms the infant initiative. Once this is properly confirmed, the baby can move on. Because there are two messages to the brain – one which tells the baby about the mother, and the other which tells the baby that its eyes are seeing or hearing or feeling the mother – it begins to feel 'self' as separate from the mother.

This is what should happen. However, if for some reason the mother or primary care giver is not able to respond or, as one might surmise in the case of ASD, the baby's brain is unable to interpret the mother's signals, the baby can fail to develop a proper sense of 'self' that is separate from 'other'. Mother and baby remain bonded in this bubble of infantile need – infant because it needs to survive, and mother because she is drawn in by the maternal instinct to meet infantile need. The mother's agenda remains the child. The baby may grow physically into adult but remains in the infantile state of critical need for the mother's nurture. It still retains the fear of extinction if it feels it is not receiving this nurture or that the 'dyad', the infant survival state, is threatened. The grown 'adult-infant' will do absolutely anything to receive the sensation of 'returning to the dyad and knowing they are receiving the mother's nurture' and the mother will do anything to satisfy this need. The direct relationship between mother and child may be replaced by 'attachment things' such as a length of string which acts as a connection, a navel cord to mother, which in turn may be replaced by other 'things'.

This is fairly rare in people on the spectrum but where it does occur the situation and care are immensely complicated. A love–hate relationship can develop between mother and child since the child's need is a black hole, a bottomless pit that can never be filled. The love is need. Negative feelings arise because mother cannot satisfy the adult-infant's need and also because the adult-infant cannot separate and is glued into the dyad. The adult-infant may break its things in order to get them replaced and momentarily re-experience the nurturing attachment sensation it so desires.

At its most difficult there is nothing in the world but 'me', as at the moment of birth. There are no boundaries, nothing but 'me, me, me' without consciousness of 'self' and 'other' – everything is swallowed in an extension of need. The world becomes a theme park designed to satisfy this need. Other people are not recognized as individuals with separate needs that need to be respected – other people are things, objects on which to act out their fantasies. Even if they have an inkling of 'persons out there', it is too dangerous to lower the barriers to reach them as to do so would be to endanger the dyadic bubble state on which their sustenance and very existence depends.

It is important to remember that we are dealing with 'feelings'. From the point of view of the outsider, the mother/adult-infant bubble 'feels' exclusive and others involved with care will feel shut out. It is difficult to cross the boundary either way – the feelings involved are so intense and primal. It requires enormous emotional effort to establish communication between the different parties involved in care since all parties will feel protective. However, a real sharing of feeling may be almost the only way to stand back and see what is happening.

Where there is separation failure, violence and aggression are common in men; women tend to be depressed. To try to establish late separation is extremely difficult – the neediness of the adult-child is so deeply embedded in the mother in the dyad. This is especially true where the situation is complicated by autism. Direct physical separation simply heightens anxiety, which sends the adult-infant back into the bubble.

The only way that can be at least partially successful is to try to find ways to raise the adult-infant's consciousness of self, at the same time as very carefully deciding what boundaries there do have to be. This also has to be negotiated with the parent involved, since they also will have difficulty in detaching themselves from the roll of 'protector to the damaged child'. Inserting such boundaries is difficult.

There are a number of ways of setting about raising self-esteem, getting a better sense of self, which I want to leave until we have looked at the problem of having a negative image, since the same approach will underlie all our therapeutic input. Basically, it will involve giving people meaningful emotional acknowledgement and confirmation.

Negative images

The NT world is so desperate to frog-march people with ASD, who it sees as damaged into the NT world that many of the messages I receive will be critical and negative. The messages that do filter through from the world out there may be so humiliating that I cannot bear what I do perceive of myself. Wendy Lawson (2003) stresses how important it is to give people positive input about themselves in order to bolster the self-esteem which flounders so easily.

Some people are not able to perceive themselves as they really are – only seeing themselves reflected in the mirror of negative comment from the world around them. They may have very poor self-esteem, to the extent that they can only talk about themselves in the third person. 'Jennie's a naughty girl' sums up their ability to define their experience of their selves. This negative image, projected by those who care for them, may not necessarily arise through deliberate hostility but simply through lack of understanding and exasperation at someone with whom they are completely unable to connect. Wendy expresses this for more able people: 'We have a tendency to be negative about ourselves. It is easier for us to believe people who are critical of us…since we see only the reality of our own failures' (Lawson 2003).

In the film *A is for Autism* (Arnall and Peters 1992) the young boy tells us how in the playground he stood and flapped his hands. All the noise made him feel as if he was going mad. He says: 'Other children thought it looked odd. They don't like kids who are odd.'

Raising self-esteem

To try to talk directly to an individual who, for whatever reason, has a displaced sense of self is like posting a letter to the wrong address. It simply does not arrive (Caldwell 2000). In order to communicate with a person who has projected their sense of self, we have to pay attention to where it is the person feels themselves to be. This will be at the site of their self-stimulus. If I scratch my fingers this may be the site of my self-awareness, where I feel that I am, because this is where I am getting my feedback from.

While this may appear to be bizarre, it is only when we recognize that our partner's reality is not the same as ours that we can begin to build up an individual's self-esteem.

Near the beginning of her book *Build Your Own Life* (2003), Wendy Lawson says that 'before [she] could venture out and explore…[her] own life, [she] needed to experience a sense of [her] own being as someone who is of value'.

This is true of all of us, autistic or NT. Therese Jolliffe tells us: 'We do love people and feel lonely' (Jolliffe *et al.* 1992).This is an extremely important statement since it runs counter to the generally perceived image of people on the autistic spectrum who are 'cold and unfeeling' and cut themselves off.

Human beings are not designed to be solitary. One of the basic human skills that we all need, or perhaps one should say basic arts, is learning to make friends. The way we go about this is to share pleasure. A very simple illustration of this arose when I was teaching a student together with a partner with ASD who spent his life rolling about the floor. If anyone came near he hit them. However, he did enjoy shiny surfaces. So the student sat on the floor with a piece of mirror paper and moved it so it caught the light. He rolled over and started to interact with her. He took the paper from her, moved it and then turned round to her, smiling over his shoulder, obviously asking her to share his pleasure. His overture was powerful, reaching back into the irresistible invitation of childhood: 'Look what I've found, come and play with me?'

We have a paradox here centred on the mistaken idea that now we are grown up we do not play – and that to use the word 'play' in an adult context is to demean our partners and treat them like children. This arises erroneously from the now discredited practice of treating adults with learning disabilities as if they were children and not according them the dignity due to adults. But at the same time we talk about valuing people, when what we are actually doing is valuing them as we think they should be rather than as they are. In learning to speak a person's inner language we show that we value them as they are – and value what they value. Not at all the same as some abstract concept of human worth which ignores the reality of who they are.

If we can show people they are important to us we can begin to raise their self-image. On a quite practical level, if we give an individual who uses third-person speech a more positive sense of self, their marginal speech may well shift to first person, sometimes quite dramatically.

A woman lives in a respite centre because her behaviour makes it difficult to find permanent accommodation. Her only speech is to call herself names. I involve her in constructing a special box in which to keep her toiletries, which are precious to her, especially as she is constantly being moved from room to room and has nowhere she can call her own. I also take photographs of her engaged in activities. These are enlarged and kept in an A4 display folder, with the aim of trying to raise her self-esteem. Her support partner goes through them with her daily, talking to her about each one. After a fortnight there is a dramatic shift in self-perception. When asked what she is doing in one, instead of using third-person speech as she had up until then ('Mary is a bad girl…'), she says, 'Don't be silly, I'm putting on my jersey.' Not only is she now speaking in the first person (having a sense of self) but is also able to defend that 'self'.

A similar change in attitude comes about in a woman with ASD and very disturbed behaviour who also talks about herself in disparaging third-person speech. She lives at home and her eyes are following her mother all the time. She is very attached to her but at the same time she has severe outbursts when she attacks her mother, but her mother says that *her daughter stops at once when she knows that she has hurt her – that is, has let out a cry of some sort.* Having experienced a similar attack on myself, with the same outcome (as soon as I responded to a blow with a cry of pain, she stopped), I was able to suggest that, in her chaotic sensory world, what it was her daughter needed so badly when she was upset was a response from her mother which penetrated her chaos but which also had significance for her. For the next day or so, I asked her mother to always respond to her non-verbal sounds (so that she was always getting a meaningful response). On the second day the young woman sat up and said, 'Shut up.' This may not be polite but her shift in self-perception enabled her to say what she wanted instead of attacking her mother. Her sense of self had altered in a palpable way and, like the woman in the previous history, she also could defend her new-found self.

Significant responses

This encounter led me to reflect that behaviour that is so often labelled as 'attention seeking' is in reality a despairing search for *significant* response – that is, one that the brain recognizes (as opposed to responses that have no meaning for the individual in question). What it actually says is 'I am desperate to be in touch with something outside myself'.

I am told that a woman is 'targeting' a member of staff, following her round all day and sniffing her hair. This type of behaviour can be very irritating and can feel very threatening from support staff's point of view. For the individual involved it may be that it is the only thing their brain recognizes and is perceived as 'safe'. In a world where little is recognizable as 'user-friendly' they are desperate for a reaction which they can actually latch on to, since most of their sensory intake is decoded as hostile (liable to initiate fragmentation). What they are looking for is confirmation, meaningful connectedness, something that actually gets through to them, penetrates the chaos. In the case of the woman who was hitting her mother it was a cry of pain which told her she had actually made connection – but it was possible to substitute sounds which were part of her own repertoire for this.

To be disconnected in this way must be like driving in thick fog. Crawling at zero speed, we need to see something beyond our windscreen wipers, a pavement, a road sign, a kerb, anything that will give us some indication of where we are. Also, as in severe autism, anything we do see is potentially dangerous since we may crash into it.

So when we work with people who have a bad self-image we need to look for ways of raising their self-esteem in ways that they recognize.

This is one of the advantages of the approach known as Intensive Inter-action. When I partner someone through using their body language, I am not trying to push them into a world that is potentially traumatic and which they can only understand at the cost of stress. When I am a partner, by joining them and using their language, I tell people that I value what they value and by implication I value them as they are, themselves as people. When they realize this their stress level comes down and they can interact more easily.

We have already discussed ways of getting emotional access through what I called a passive acceptance approach when working with bad language. As we know, the normal response to this is to try to stop the person using it. It was pointed out that bad language, however offensive we may find it, is actually an indication of an emotional state. If we ignore or repress it we are actually denying the person how they feel. What is effective is if we acknowledge the state. In order to work, this has to use the *actual word* in order to confirm the adult-infant and allow them to move on. Sympathy is not enough. The actual message that we send them is that 'I respect how you as a person are feeling – and, by implication, you are a worthwhile person'.

Another approach used successfully with a woman who had a very low self-image and was extremely disturbed was to involve her in her own behavioural control. We devised a 'yellow' card system. Both the person and those supporting her had a yellow card which they could hold up if they thought the situation was getting fraught. This was the signal for those around her to withdraw so that all could have space to cool off. Everyone sat down. What was essential was that the woman herself was responsible for seeing that she and all who visited, and those who supported her, were issued with a card. She collected and distributed them. This gave her control and thereby valued her as a person. The exact threshold for holding up the yellow card needed to be early on the escalation scale.

I want to come back now to the people for whom this book is written. Christopher, Pranve and Gabriel are intrinsically valuable people, valuable as they are now. They may never perhaps reach the same cognitive potential as they might have had if they did not have ASD but this does not take away from their value as unique individuals, their flavour. The problem of recognition is ours. How can I show them that I truly value what they value? When Gabriel flicks his string, how can I abandon my own world (where string-flicking is not viewed as an adult or productive or even interesting activity) and show him I really do enjoy what he does? I doubt if I shall get away with feigned interest. A cognitive decision to pretend that I value it is not going to be good enough. I cannot be convincing unless I really am prepared to drop my indifference to string-flicking as an occupation and start to care about it. There is no room for boredom or nagging doubts that I am looking silly or wasting my time.

So I am going to start any interventions with the following beliefs:

1.   People are in themselves inherently valuable.

2.   There is a biological imperative to make friends.

3.   The way we make friends is through sharing.

4.   Sharing increases my sensory awareness.

5.   Through shared sensory awareness we become aware of each other as people.

6.   Through learning about each other we learn about ourselves.

Or, to put it simply, it is the sharing that is important. The string-flicking is a vehicle for our shared attention, not the primary centre of attention. But, paradoxically, it is through paying attention to 'flicking' that I get a deepening sense of its physical attributes and qualia (quality as perceived by me – for example, the 'greenness' of green). Gabriel shows me qualities of experience and different sensations that I should not have come to otherwise and this leads me to true sharing. It's not just a one-way ticket, me giving to him. As I discover, I receive as well as give. This is what equality is really about, not just an external passport to the same facilities, important though this is. Flicking (in this case) is a means to an end, which is the infinitely valuable experience of 'other'.

And this also brings me to the realization that if I am really going to value you, I need to find you Christopher, you Pranve and you Gabriel, as much as you need to find me, for in doing so I shall find myself. And you cannot find me unless I am really present to you. In other words we shall both get something out of our partnership. This is not just about playing with string but the underlying and unbelievably important two-way human activity of building a relationship. I am honoured to learn your language and talk to you. I learn that the equality we talk about so much is not just me handing down my so-called understanding. True equality is when we both understand each other's emotional language and I enjoy and learn from my partner as they do from me. In being for each other we become ourselves.

Gabriel and the dyad

In the training video *Learning the Language* (Caldwell 2002b), we watch the change in Gabriel's behaviour, from isolation to interaction over a period of two days (actually about five hours' interaction). What we see is more than just a behavioural change. As Gabriel moves from the picture we first see of him, beating his head on the cupboard door, through the development of attention and engagement, what we are witnessing is the emergence of a man with a sense of self, one which he radiantly enjoys sharing with other. Before we start to examine this in detail, I should like to point out that it raises the question of how it is that we can witness such a change. How is it that a person who cannot ever make eye contact can rise above this to deep gaze?

At about the same time as he starts shaking his string and then looking to see if I will answer him, his body posture relaxes. He lifts his head and looks around the room calmly, looking at his surroundings in a way we have not seen before, reminding me of Donna Williams' surprise when she first put on her glasses: 'My God, that's what the rest of the world has been seeing' (Williams 1999).

The confused/withdrawn look has gone and he is no longer cut off. He continues to play with his string but in a way that is not so frantic. He smiles to himself quietly, amused by something – but his amusement is not secret because he is prepared to look out and share it. When he stops pacing he stands close to me, looks quizzically at me and then turns round to see what others are making of this. I follow him and we end up standing close to each other. His smile has broken through so that his face is beaming as he gazes deep into my eyes and I into his.

The glass bubble

This mutual gaze is so moving. It is a feature we first come across in the mother–infant bonding when parent and child gaze at each other, lost in each other's presence. It is as if they are closed off in a glass bubble. Outsiders may say they feel left out, 'excluded'. Within the boundary Lonergan points out that 'the self is lifted from self-consciousness'. We also see this in adults when they are in love but, as Suzanne Zeedyk points out, whereas it feels all right to observe mother and child involved in what is known as a dyadic episode where two partners are totally engaged with each other, gazing into each other's eyes, lost to the world, when we witness it between adults, even in these desensitized days, there is a feeling of being a voyeur and we are inclined to tiptoe away and let them get on with it (Zeedyk 2005). A colleague tells me that someone who watched the *Learning the Language* video (Caldwell 2002b) said, 'How can she get so close?' (She meant in a psychological sense – at no time were we touching.)

It is as if one's affect (emotional perception) has itself become mutual. There is no longer 'I' and 'you'; the felt experience is of 'we'. The paradox is that at this time one is more powerfully aware of 'self' in a new way. Time stops. A student once told me that what I was speaking of was known as 'flow'. Flow lasts 'as long as we have got' (Lubbock 2002) – and also for as long as we can cope with it – since affect is so powerful that, in the end, courtesy leads us to turn away. But we are not the same. Something has been exchanged. We are changed, both of us.

Our eyes are our windows. We use them to see. But the use we make of this gift of sight is largely determined by our intent. Even when our eyes are wide open, the shutters of our mind may be closed if we are not relating to what we see. Under these circumstances we should say, 'she looked blank'. The person is cut off from us. Either unconsciously or consciously, there is no intent to interact. In order to look, we have to open the shutters to take in what is going on around us. Even then, we can look without communicating unless we make a decision to let 'other' into 'self'.

Gaze is different. Not only do the facial muscles relax but here we have moved beyond our cognitive territory into the poetic terrain of 'drink to me only with thine eyes', from sight to sensation. Recent work suggests that it is just possible that this is exactly what is happening.

A doctor, age 52, has recently had two strokes which have left him 'cortically blind'. This means that although his eyes and optic nerve are functioning normally, the normal cortical system for processing what he sees is no longer working. All that he does see is darkness. Nevertheless he scores better than average when undergoing tests designed to recognize facial emotions such as fear, joy, hate, etc. which are flashed up on a computer screen. Scans indicate that during the part of the test when he is 'guessing emotions', his brain is using an alternative route. The stimuli that cannot be processed through the cortex are now routed through the amygdala. However, this does not allow him to process non-emotional visual features. What this tells us is that the amygdala, a small walnut-sized area of the brain previously thought to be only processing fear, is an alternative route to processing through the cortex. It is capable of undertaking visual processing for a range of emotions, through a process known as 'blindsight' (Pegna *et al.* 2005).

Speculation suggests that, possibly, when we look into the eyes of another in the dyadic state – and exchange 'seeing' for 'perception', when we see nothing but are aware of everything – we may have thrown the switch from cortical processing to amygdala processing with all the hormonal possibilities of change.

To come back to Gabriel and autism, I can see the objection that people with ASD cannot read faces. Yet witnessing the prolonged in-depth bonding in the dyadic experience, under these circumstances this seems to be precisely what is happening. This can be seen clearly in the training video *Learning the Language* (Caldwell 2002b). This experience with Gabriel is not a one-off, it is not such an uncommon event, although usually it quickly slides off and resolves into a hug. However, with people with ASD, such profound bonding only seems to be possible when we have already entered each other's world through learning and interacting through each other's inner language. We have used their personal code to get access to their inner world without triggering the fight/flight response.

It is not easy to hold someone's gaze like this. In a way touching would be an easier option – with adults the gaze would normally be resolved through embrace. When I find myself drawn in to the dyad, in order to hold it, I need not only to open the shutters of my mind but also to draw back the inner curtain. I do this by consciously emptying myself and allowing the inflow to happen. It is a question not only of presence but giving and receiving. I have to let my partner share myself as I share myself with my partner. This is what we mean by bonding.

In some ways the term 'dyad' is used rather loosely and I should like to distinguish between being a partner and the dyadic experience. There are three possibilities.

1. Partner-to-partner duo. The partnership should always be one of mutual interest and co-operation. It has the potential to lead into the dyadic state.

2. Gaze-seeker-to-partner couple. Here, one half of the partnership seeks gaze while the other does not know how to accept this. The relationship is lopsided and out of sync. A partner who is not used to opening up will observe the gaze but not allow it to come into them. Not knowing what to do with it can be embarrassing – one feels awkward and from the spectator's viewpoint it looks markedly awkward. Experience and learning to make the conscious decision to allow another into self does eventually make such bonding easier. For one thing the power of the dyadic flow does not come as such a shock.

3. The dyad. The switch from looking to mutual inner gaze is complete. Both partners are totally involved with each other to the exclusion of outsiders. Sight is replaced by affect.

Just as with the mother–child dyad, I would suggest that the surge of sensation associated with bonding is probably linked to the hormone oxytocin (OT), the 'feel-good' hormone, which is also involved in infant–mother attachment. OT has the potential to reorganize brain function and moderate behavioural responses. The release of OT is associated with a reduction in anxiety (Carter 2003; Hollander *et al.* 2003; Modahl *et al.* 1998). Also I should further suggest that this is at least one of the factors involved in the positive changes in behaviour witnessed by those involved in Intensive Interaction.

Within the dyad there is total attention, vulnerability, profound respect for the partner as they are, simultaneous awareness of other and self within the partnership, tenderness and a flow of pure affect. To borrow a phrase from Malouf, 'the language we speak now is the language where every syllable is a gesture of reconciliation' (Malouf 1978).

We who are NT may find it difficult to believe that we are sharing this profound human experience with someone who is labelled as having autism, which by definition sets our partner up as a person apart, one with whom those of us who are NT cannot connect. Why should this be so surprising? They are people as we are. All that has happened is that we have opened up an alternative route to communication, in particular a route that does not involve interpretation. Now we can be with each other without triggering the defensive systems. Here we are together. Although we shall not always experience this degree of connectedness with our partner, when we do we shall never feel the same about them again. They have in some sense become part of us and, it is hoped, we of them, although the only indications we have of this are their evident pleasure and calmness.

Separation

We cannot live in the high dyad however much we might like to. In order to help our partners grow, we need to try and use every opportunity to bolster their new-found sense of self. Everything we do with them must be aimed at enlarging the positive image they have now found. We have to enter into their world and by using their language show them that we value what they value. We will find our own values changed.

Simple strategies move us from controlling their lives to giving them control. The hardest bit is that we need to change how we think – we need to prioritize negotiation and interaction above activity, so that whatever we do is a matter of mutual assent. This involves training ourselves so that throughout our daily lives we are constantly referring back to our partners, making sure that we are in agreement over whatever option is being offered, using body language where necessary. We have to learn the difference between being directive and task-orientated, and being engaged, which is person-orientated and involves a much closer level of interaction.

For example, person-centred plans may give an overall picture of what a person likes to do or not do but they do not tell us if they want to do this particular activity today, now. Real engagement has to focus on an intimate connection with the present.

Management and staff may feel threatened by the implication that 'talk' is more important than 'walk', that communication and relationship have priority over programmes. They will ask how they can possibly organize their lives if they cannot keep to timetables. Sometimes they will object that such an approach will mean a whole new way of looking at how they work. (But at the same time they are worrying about the very serious behavioural problems that their current practice is in essence promoting.)

And in some ways they are right. However, even more difficult is that as well as work practices, the change may also require us to look at a different way of viewing our own values and how we relate to others. A training officer said that such an approach takes the meaning of being 'person-centred' onto a different level.

The way to go about this is not so much to think in terms of 'doing Intensive Interaction' but to allow interaction to be part of our natural daily communication. Everything we do together becomes a vehicle for interaction. Using body language becomes just part of the way we talk to and spend time with each other. The whole approach is about 'learning to be with', rather than 'doing'. If we are able to make this turnaround, somewhat to our awkward surprise we will find that within the parameters of their hypersensitivities, people with autism also want to live normal lives. Once we have relinquished our need to control and learned their language they can feel safe enough to trust us. As their confidence grows, so too will ours. We can grow together in rewarding mutual partnership. Oh yes – and have fun together.

Coda

This book set out to explore the lives of people who are known as being on the autistic spectrum and whose interpretation of the reality we all share is different from those of us who are NT. In particular it looks at those people in this group whose cognitive faculties are impaired, so that they have little or no way of picking up the pieces and rationalizing their way out of the turmoil which is their life experience. In their distress, those who are least able retreat into their own worlds and may become deeply disturbed when they perceive a threat to that sanctuary.

But the paradox here is summed up by a teacher who uses Intensive Interaction and said to me recently that she was surprised by how often she came across joy. I agree with her and would go further. This joy is not something we can do by ourselves – it is found in sharing, something we experience together. Valuing someone is not an intellectual intent but a discovery – that we find ourselves, 'become' in each other. No matter how able or disabled, NT or autistic we are, we can do this for and with each other and ourselves. If we allow ourselves to be present for each other, this is the great human prize. Each time we bring joy to each other we are honoured.

The Causes of ASD

In spite of all information coming out at present about autistic spectrum disorder (ASD), it has not been possible so far to pin down its origin to one specific cause. It is very probable that what we are calling autism arises from multiple causes. For example, if we look at diet, in a sample of 230 people tried on the wheat-free/milk-free diet, the symptoms of 17 were considerably moderated – but no difference was observed in the rest. Here is a sub-group of people with ASD whose symptoms do not appear to have the same immediate cause as those of other people who also present as having ASD (Hinton 2003).

When looking at the conflicting theories it is important to distinguish between cause and effect – much of which is popularly being described as cause is almost certainly outcome, not aetiology. The autism question is about numbers. Is there really a big increase?

What is now clear is that when we talk about what we see as autism, we are talking about neurobiological damage and not, as was once thought, uncaring parenting. In our brains we have something like a trillion nerve connections. The nerves (neurons), which transmit messages along themselves electrically, do not actually touch each other at the junctions where they meet. The gaps are called synapses. The gaps between these branched neurons are bridged by chemical messengers, known as 'neurotransmitters'. Something like 80 different neuro-transmitters have been identified so far and to a large extent the balance between them determines our reactions.

At present there are a number of different suggested underlying causes which may or may not link together. First, there is in many cases a genetic link, possibly as high as 80 per cent. More than one gene is likely to be involved, perhaps as many as four. Certainly there are families in which there is more than one member who has ASD.

Baron-Cohen et al. (1985) have measured the level of testosterone in the mother's womb and subsequently followed the development of these children, who are now around five years old. Their conclusion is that where there is too much testosterone in the womb, the infant is at risk of having difficulties forming relationships and learning skills such as reading and writing.

Then there is the suggestion that autism is linked with the triple injection known as MMR (measles, mumps and rubella). The most convincing argument against such a link is provided by the results of the recent Japanese survey of 30,000 children since the use of the triple injection was halted in 1993. Since discontinuation, the number of children diagnosed with ASD has continued to rise, doubling since the MMR injection was withdrawn. If there was a link it would have been expected to fall.

However, there are still puzzling clusters which seem unlikely to have arisen by chance. One such concerns a family whose two boys are separated by three years. Both developed normally until they reached the age of three when, three years apart, they were given the triple injection. In both cases they started to present as typically autistic within 24 hours of receiving it. It is difficult to maintain that this arose by chance. The most likely explanation is that in this and similar cases the family have a genetic disposition which predisposes them to be particularly sensitive to the intervention. If this were the case, the relatively small number of families in which this is a factor might be the reason they do not appear as statistically significant – but nevertheless critical for the families involved.

Meg Megson (2004), a Canadian paediatrician, suggests that damage to the G-proteins leads to faults in the 'rods' in the retina of the eye. If this is so, it would explain a great deal about the visual problems so commonly experienced by people with ASD. The rods are responsible for processing red and green and also depth. Any fault in these would explain the lack of stability in the visual field, where perceived objects slither around. People describe it as like living in a kaleidoscope where the pattern never settles.

In particular, the use of MRI and fMRI scanners has given a new and powerful way of investigating what could previously only be surmised from behaviour. A trawl through *ScienceDaily* (www.sciencedaily.com/releases) discusses the link between ASD and tuberous sclerosis, where ASD is a common occurrence. Biochemical abnormalities in the brain's outer layer (the cortex) have a major impact on communication skills, whereas changes in sub-cortical regions were associated with the development of stereotypical behaviours and lack of social interaction (Chugani 2001). Other areas of research are looking at:

1. evidence of inflammation of the brains of some people with autism and its association with activation of the brain's immune system (Pardo-Villamizar 2004)

2. a ten per cent increase in cerebral volume as compared both with NT brains and with children with developmental delay (Dager 2002)

3. an increased number of smaller 'minicolumns' (a basic organizational unit of brain cells and connective wiring that effect processing) in the brains of people with ASD, the effect of which would be to keep the brain in a constant state of over-arousal and make it harder to discriminate between competing sensory information (Casanova 2002)

4. left-brain/right-brain differences in a comparison between high-functioning people with ASD and NT people, with the autistic group showing more activity in the right-hand brain than the left as opposed to the NT group – the left-hand hemisphere is associated with processing verbal information and the right with visual and spacial information processing (Koshina 2004).

The brain is infinitely complex and we have to wait a little longer before the neurochemistry and brain structures associated with specific behaviours in ASD can be clarified.

The Japanese study alone indicates a massive increase in children receiving a diagnosis of autism but there is still no agreement as to whether this is due to an actual increase or different patterns of diagnosis. However, on an anecdotal scale, teachers nearing the end of their career compare the one or two children with ASD a year they used to take in to school with the three or four a term who may come in now, which, since they are not responsible for any change in the way children are diagnosed, does indicate a real increase.

APPENDIX B

The Way In – Using Intensive Interaction

In order to practise Intensive Interaction, we have to think of the person we are working with as our partner. We start with looking at our partner's body language, how they are self-stimulating, and use the sounds and movements they are making to talk to themselves – their own inner language – as a way of communication with them.

First of all we need to put aside our own expectations and agenda since these may well prevent our seeing what is actually happening.

We need to observe everything they are doing intently. We have to observe extremely carefully not just their face (which is where we are used to looking) but also at all their bodily movements and changes in posture. We need to give our partner total attention, listen for any sound, even those we should normally ignore such as breathing rhythm, sucking saliva, grinding teeth or the explosive sound at the end of breath holding. We want to know which sensations of the body our partner is attending to, how they are talking to themselves and which signals form part of their familiar landscape which the brain will recognize.

We start with observation to see:

- *what* a person is doing – what sensory feedback are they giving themselves?

- *how* are they doing it – how a person is waving their hands or making a sound will tell us about *how they feel*, their emotional state, whether they are calm/upset.

- *where* (exactly) they are stimulating themselves – very often they may be so focused on the particular location of a self-stimulus that they may not respond to a direct approach.

Once we see what they are doing, we gradually join in, using trial and error, observing carefully their reactions to our interventions. When we identify what it is that our partner is attending to, the next stage is to try to use an element of their language to talk to them. When they make a sound or movement, we answer them. We are trying to establish that every time they do something they will get a response from the world outside that is meaningful for them. The communication partner echoes back the behaviour of the person they are working with – but what they are aiming for is not exact copying or imitation. Rather, their aim is to learn how the person talks to themselves and to enter into dialogue with them. We have to learn the language which has meaning for their brain. We are responding, not mimicking.

Some people will feel 'silly' waving their hands or making non-verbal noises. If we feel self-conscious it is because we are thinking about ourselves and not our partner, worrying about what other people will think about us. We need to keep our attention focused on and in the person we are working with.

When our partner recognizes 'their sound' or 'their movement', attention shifts from their inner world of self-stimulation to the world outside, looking for the source of an initiative which they recognize but did not make themselves. It is surprise that induces the attention shift: 'That was my sound (or my movement) but I didn't do it, or it sounds a bit different', etc.

Each person will indicate the attention shift in a different way. They may simply move their eyes to look in the direction of the source, or move their head or their body. Occasionally if they are partially deaf, they may turn their head away to present their 'best' ear. Their eyes may 'light up' with pleasure and they may smile, laugh or move forward to an embrace. Alternatively, all we may notice is a change in tension as the body posture alters very slightly. We know that they are listening to us.

Once our partner knows that when they make an initiative they will get a response, we can start to build up a conversation, taking turns and using their sounds and movements in a creative way. In order to widen our engagement, we no longer copy our partner exactly but use elements of their language put together in different ways to respond to their initiatives. This creates more surprise. When we see an action which may not be an exact copy but relates to our action we also recognize it. Even if it is not exactly the same, when the brain compares the incoming image with its own repertoire, it finds that the 'copy' contains vital elements of its original. The brain is expecting one input and it gets it – but there's a difference. It is this surprise which is intriguing and our partner's attention hardens into engagement. At the same time they will start to introduce new material and then refer back to see what we make of it. (It is extremely important not to miss this since if we do we send the message that we are not listening to them.)

Timing is critical. Our partners may need time to process a reply and we must give them space to do so. It is very important not to rush into a space but wait and see what they will do. We need to be careful not to overload them. (The responses of a person with ASD may take a long time to organize – hours, even sometimes a day or so. This is very much a feature of people with Fragile X Syndrome. They know what they want to say but cannot manage to formulate it. Sometimes they may feel very threatened during this interval, especially if the pressure is piled on as we try to help them answer – it can add to the confusion. It is vital that we learn to wait, sometimes for much longer than we feel is natural for us.)

Many people with ASD feel threatened if people stand too close to them or look them in the eye or demand emotional warmth. When working with such individuals we must take care to stand back and if necessary look away from them instead of at them. Sometimes it is better to sit beside them rather than opposite.

Some people with ASD will also have visual or hearing impairments. We must be sure that we position ourselves so that responses to movement are within their visual or auditory field but at the same time respect any need they may have for personal space. As with those who cannot hear us, we may need to draw or tap the rhythm of sounds or movements on someone who cannot see our responses so we need to find out where they can tolerate touch, such as on the back, upper arm or foot. Occasionally they will reject touch altogether. Our response here might be to blow on their face or scratch or tap or bang the chair so that they feel our answer without touch. A man with ASD who has no sight, and serious behavioural problems, licks his lips in a circular movement. He will not allow touch on his body except on the upper surface of his foot. I draw the pattern of his movements on his foot and he laughs, especially when I add a little surprise by changing the direction of the circles. No-one has heard him laugh before. We can always find some way to let people know that when they do something we will reply.

Some people with ASD will have epilepsy. Support staff need training to recognize and be aware of the significance of absences or other seizures. *Occasionally*, over-excitement can trigger overload or a seizure. If this is a problem, the time and level of interactions need to be reduced.

We have to be especially careful never to 'hype people up'. We need to work towards centring our interactions, always listening to the emotional content of their communications and bringing quiet empathy to our sounds. Using our voice to answer a partner may involve lifting it towards the end of a sound in order to ask a question: 'Is this how it feels?' The aim is always to put ourselves alongside our partner.

It is absolutely essential that we work from whatever our partner is doing *now*, and not use the material we had such a good time using together yesterday. That is yesterday's conversation and tells our partner we are not listening to them today. It is very easy to slip into the practice of 'this is the game we play with John'. John may find it fun at first but his brain will get used to the sameness and it will get bored. As he becomes habituated his attention will slip back into his inner world.

If our partner becomes deeply engaged in our face we need to learn to accept this sensitive desire to know us more profoundly – and willingly open our selves to their gaze.

If touch is used as a means of communication there needs to be a written management strategy that support staff have read and signed. This is for the protection of both partners. I often get asked how long we should go on working with people, to which the answer is: how long is a conversation? The question of how long we talk to each other is an individual one. Some people with ASD can only manage quite a short time before they get overloaded. Ideally, Intensive Interaction becomes just part of the way we relate to people; it is a vehicle like speech which we use to convey our feelings and learn to enjoy each other's company.

Teamwork is essential. All members of a support circle need to learn to develop their interactive skills as there is a danger of a person becoming fixated on a particular member of the team if they are the only partners they have. We need to share information, especially that which concerns an individual's particular sensitivities.

Snoezelen – use of the sensory room

- The sensory room should be used to promote interaction.
- *Think before use.* What stimulus does this person particularly respond to?
- Explore one sense at a time. Try using just one source.
- Explore it with the client(s).
- If that is successful, try a related source, based on the same type of stimulus.
- *Never go in and switch everything on.* It is too confusing in sensory terms.
- Do not have the radio on unless it is being used to explore sound.
- The whole point of Snoezelen is to be able to isolate and explore individual sensory experiences. As it is currently being used, the opposite is happening. The senses are being bombarded with an overload of stimuli.
- Remember that although a person with ASD may be fascinated by a particular piece of equipment, this will not necessarily help them to interact. It is finding ways to interact on a personal level which has the potential for changing lives.

References

Arnall, D. and Peters, J. (1992) *A is for Autism*. London: A Finetake Production for BBC Radio 4.

Astafiev, S.V., Stanley, C.M., Shulman, G.L. and Corbetta, M. (2004) 'Extrastriate body area in human occipital cortex responds to the performance of motor actions.' *Nature Neuroscience 7*, 542–548.

Baron-Cohen, S., Leslie, A. and Frith, U. (1985) 'Does the autistic child have a theory of mind?' *Cognition 21*, 37–46.

Barron, J. and Barron, S. (1992) *There's a Boy in Here*. New York: Simon and Schuster.

Beardon, L. (2004) 'Autism, Diversity and Individuality.' Paradigm Conference, Sheffield Hallam University, October.

Blackburn, R. (2004) Flint NAS Seminar. July.

Butterworth, G. (1991) 'The ontogeny and phylogeny of joint visual attention.' In A. Whiten (ed) *Natural Theories of Mind: Evolution, Development and Simulation of Everyday Mindreading*. Oxford: Blackwell.

Caldwell, P. (1998) *Person to Person*. Brighton: Pavilion Publishing.

Caldwell, P. (2000) *You Don't Know What It's Like*. Brighton: Pavilion Publishing.

Caldwell, P. (2002a) *Crossing the Minefield*. Brighton: Pavilion Publishing.

Caldwell, P. (2002b) *Learning the Language*. Training video. Brighton: Pavilion Publishing.

Caldwell, P. (2005) *Creative Conversations*. Training video. Brighton: Pavilion Publishing.

Carter, C.S. (2003) 'Developmental consequences of oxytocin.' *Physiology and Behaviour 79*, 383–397.

Carter, R. (1998) *Mapping the Mind*. London: Phoenix.

Casanova, M.F. (2002) 'Abnormalities in brains of autism patients.' *Science Daily*, 13 February, online.

Chugani, D.C. (2001) 'Autistic behaviour linked to several brain areas in children with tuberous sclerosis.' *Neurology*, 10 October, online.

Coia, P. (2004) Private communication. Consultant Psychiatrist, Fieldhead Hospital, Wakefield.

Dager, S.R. (2002) 'Early brain growth and autism.' *Science Daily*, 24 July, online.

Damasio, A.R. (1994) *Descartes' Error: Emotion, Reason and the Human Brain*. New York: G.P. Putnam.

Davidson, R. *et al.* (2005) 'Eye contact triggers threat signals in autistic children's brains.' *Nature Neuroscience*, 6 March.

Dawson, G. and Galpert, L. (1990) 'Mother's use of imitative play for facilitating social responsiveness and toy play in young children.' *Development and Psychopathology 2*, 151–162.

Durie, B. (2005) 'Senses special: Doors of perception.' *New Scientist*, 29 January.

Emblem, B. *et al.* (1998) 'The challenge of class six.' In D. Hewett (ed) *Challenging Behaviour.* London: David Fulton Publishers.

Ephraim, G. (1986) *A Brief Introduction to Augmented Mothering.* Radlett: Harperbury Hospital School.

Gedye, A. (1989) 'Episodic rage and aggression attributed to frontal lobe seizures.' *Journal of Mental Deficiency Research 33,* 369–379.

Gerland, G. (1996) *A Real Person.* London: Souvenir Press.

Gervais, H., Pascal, B., Boddaert, N., Leboyer, M., Coez, A., Sfaello, I., Barthelemy, C., Brunelle, F., Samson, Y. and Zilbovicius, M. (2004) 'Abnormal cortical voice processing in autism.' Advance online publication. *Nature Neuroscience,* July.

Gillingham, G. (1995) *Autism – Handle with Care.* Alberta: Tacit Publishing.

Gillingham, G. (2000) *Autism – A New Understanding.* Alberta: Tacit Publishing.

Grandin, T. (1995) *Thinking in Pictures.* New York: Doubleday.

Grandin, T. and Scariano, M. (1986) *Emergence Labelled Autistic.* New York: Warner.

Hart, P. (2004) 'Using Imitation with Congenitally DeafBlind People.' British Psychological Society Developmental Section Conference, Leeds, September.

Hewett, D. (2005) GAP Conference: Valuing Good Practice in Autism, Reading, March.

Hinton, S. (2003) Private communication.

Hobson, P. (2002) *The Cradle of Thought.* Basingstoke: Macmillan.

Hollander, E., Novotny, S., Hanratty, M., Yaffe, R., DeCaria, C., Aronowitz, B. and Mosovich, S. (2003) 'Oxytocin infusion reduces repetitive behaviour in adults with autistic and Asperger's syndrome.' *Neuropsychopharmacology 28,* 193–198.

Hughes, R. (2003) *Running with Walker: A Memoir.* London: Jessica Kingsley Publishers.

Jolliffe, T., Lansdown, R. and Robinson, C. (1992) 'Autism: A personal account.' *Communication 26,* 3. [Copies of paper available from the NAS.]

Jordon, R. (2001) *Autism and Severe Learning Difficulties.* London: Souvenir Press.

Kohler, E., Keysers, C., Umiltà, M.A., Fogassi, L., Gallese, V. and Rizzolatti, G. (2002) 'Hearing sounds, understanding actions: action representation in mirror neurons.' *Science 297,* 5582, 846–848.

Koshina, H. (2004) 'Left brain/right brain differences in people with autism.' *Science Daily,* 7 December, online.

Kugiumatzakis, J.E. (1993) 'Intersubjective vocal imitation in early mother–infant interaction.' In A. Nadel and L. Camaioni (eds) *New Perspectives in Early Communicative Development.* London: Routledge.

Lawson, W. (2003) *Build Your Own Life: A Self-Help Guide for Individuals with Asperger Syndrome.* London: Jessica Kingsley Publishers.

Lewes, G. (2003) *Keeping Mum.* Tarset: Bloodaxe.

Lubbock, T. (2002) 'Rich creations of patience.' *Independent,* 2 July.

Malouf, D. (1978) *An Imaginary Life.* London: Chatto and Windus.

Megson, M. (2004) www.Megson.com

Meltzoff, A.N. (1999) 'Origins of theory of mind, cognition and communication.' *Journal of Communication Disorders 32,* 251–269.

Meltzoff, A.N. and Moore, M.K. (1992) 'Early imitation within a functional framework: the importance of person identity, movement and development.' *Infant Behaviour and Development 15*, 479–505.

Meltzoff, A.N. and Moore, M.K. (1994) 'Imitation, memory and the representation of persons.' *Infant Development and Behaviour 17*, 83–99.

Meltzoff, A.N. and Moore, M.K. (1995) 'A theory of the role of imitation in the emergence of self.' In P. Rochat (ed) *The Self in Infancy: Theory and Research.* Amsterdam: Elsevier.

Modahl, C., Green, L., Fein, D., Morris, M. *et al.* (1998) 'Plasma oxytocin levels in autistic children.' *Biological Psychiatry 42*, 270–277.

Nadel, J. and Camaioni, L. (1993) *New Perspectives in Early Communicative Development.* London: Routledge.

Nadel, J. and Peze, A. (1993) 'What makes imitation communicative in toddlers and children with autism?' In J. Nadel and L. Camaioni (eds) *New Perspectives in Early Communication.* London: Routledge.

Nadel, J., Revel, A., Andry, P. and Gaussier, P. (2004) 'Towards communication: first imitations in infants, low-functioning children with autism and robots.' *Interaction Studies, Social Behaviour and Communication in Biological and Artificial Systems 5*, 1.

Nafstad, A. and Rodbroe, I. (1999) *Co-creating Communication.* Oslo: Forlaget-Nord Press.

Nagy, E. and Molnar, P. (2004) 'Homo imitans or homo provocans? Human imprinting model of neonatal imitation.' *Infant Behaviour and Development 27*, 1, 54–63.

Nind, M. and Hewett, D. (1994) *Access to Communication.* London: David Fulton Publishers.

Nind, M. and Hewett, D. (2001) *A Practical Guide to Intensive Interaction.* Kidderminster: BILD.

Oberman, L.M., Hubbard, E.M., McCleery, J.P., Altschuler, E., Vilayanur, S., Ramachandran, V.S. and Pineda, J.A. (2005) 'EEG evidence for mirror neuron dysfunction in autism spectrum disorders.' *Cognitive Brain Research 24*, 2, 190–198.

O'Brian, L. (2004) 'My Story.' Paradigm Conference. October.

Pardo-Villamizar, C. (2004) 'Brain's immune system triggered in autism.' *ScienceDaily*, 17 November, online.

Pauli, D. (2003) Birmingham University Education Department. Ph.D. Thesis.

Peeters, T. (1997) *Autism – From Theoretical Understanding to Educational Intervention.* London: Whurr Publishers.

Pegna, A., Khatab, A., Lazeyras, F. and Seghier, M. (2005) 'Discriminating emotional faces without primary visual cortices involves the right amygdala.' *Nature Neuroscience 8*, 1, 24–25.

Rankin, K. (2000) *Growing Up Severely Autistic – They Call Me Gabriel.* London: Jessica Kingsley Publishers.

Reddy, V., Hay, M.D., Murray, L. and Trevarthen, C. (1997) 'Communication in infancy. Mutual regulation of affect and attention.' In G. Bremner and A. Slater (eds) *Infant Development: Recent Advances.* Hove: Erlbaum.

Rizzolatti, G. and Arbib, M. (1998) 'Language within our grasp.' *Trends in Neuroscience 21*, 188–194.

Rizzolatti, G., Camarda, R., Gallese, V. and Fogassi, L. (1995) 'Premotor recognition of motor actions.' *Cognitive Brain Research 3*, 131–141.

Rodbroe, I. (2004) Dundee–Bergen University Seminar. Private communication.

Seyburt, J. (2002) Maryland Coalition for Inclusive Education, Baltimore Convention Center.

Trevarthen, C. (2001) 'Intrinsic motives for companionship in understanding: their origin, development and significance for infant mental health.' *Infant Mental Health Journal 22*, 95–131.

Weeks, L. (Undated) *A Bridge of Voices.* Documentary audiotape, BBC Radio 4. Produced by Tom Morton for Sandprint Programs.

Williams, D. (1995) *Jam Jar.* Channel 4 programme. Glasgow, Scotland: Fresh Film and Television.

Williams, D. (1996) *Autism – An Inside-Out Approach.* London: Jessica Kingsley Publishers.

Williams, D. (1998) *Autism and Sensing: The Unlost Instinct.* London: Jessica Kingsley Publishers.

Williams, D. (1999a) *Nobody Nowhere: The Remarkable Autobiography of an Autistic Girl.* London: Jessica Kingsley Publishers.

Williams, D. (1999b) *Somebody Somewhere: Breaking Free from the World of Autism.* London: Jessica Kingsley Publishers.

Williams, J.H.G., Whiten, A., Suddendorf, T. and Perrett, D.I. (2001) 'Imitation, motor neurones and autism.' *Neuroscience and Behavioural Reviews 25*, 287–295.

Zeedyk, M.S. (2005) 'From intersubjectivity to subjectivity.' *Infant and Child Development*, in press.

Resources

Seminar on hyperacusis: M. Brown, Consultant Audiologist, Royal Lancaster Infirmary, Ashton Road, Lancaster, Lancashire LA1 4RP.

Irlen Centre East, 4 Park Farm Business Centre, Fornham St Genevieve, Bury St Edmunds, Suffolk, IP28 6TS. Tel: 01284 724301.

TEACCH, Autism Independent UK (formerly SFTAH), 199–205 Blandford Avenue, Kettering, Northants, NN16 9AT.

Arnall, D. and Peters, J. (1992) *A is for Autism.* London: A Finetake production for BBC Radio 4.

Caldwell, P. (2002) *Learning the Language.* Training video. Brighton: Pavilion Publishing. Video covering the establishment of communication with a man with very severe ASD who was not responding to alternative approaches.

Caldwell, P. (2005) *Creative Conversations.* Training video. Brighton: Pavilion Publishing. Although this video is about people with multiple disability, it also contains a discussion on the use of Intensive Interaction.

Caldwell, P. (2004) 'Can We Talk?' Free simplified and illustrated handout on autism on www.nwtdt.com.

Damasio, A.R. (1999) *The Feeling of What Happens.* London: Heinemann.

Williams, D. (1999) *Like Colour to the Blind: Soul Searching and Soul Finding.* London: Jessica Kingsley Publishers.

Williams, D. (2003) *Exposure Anxiety: The Invisible Cage.* London: Jessica Kingsley Publishers.

Subject Index

Author Index